U. S. DEPARTMENT
OF TRANSPORTATION
FEDERAL AVIATION
ADMINISTRATION

WILDLIFE STRIKES
TO CIVIL AIRCRAFT
IN THE
UNITED STATES
1990–2008

U. S. Department
of Agriculture
Animal and Plant
Health Inspection
Service
Wildlife Services

FEDERAL AVIATION ADMINISTRATION
NATIONAL WILDLIFE STRIKE DATABASE
SERIAL REPORT NUMBER 15

I0438704

REPORT OF THE ASSOCIATE ADMINISTRATOR OF AIRPORTS
OFFICE OF AIRPORT SAFETY AND STANDARDS
AIRPORT SAFETY & CERTIFICATION
WASHINGTON, DC

SEPTEMBER 2009

The Federal Aviation Administration produced this report in cooperation with the U. S. Department of Agriculture, Animal and Plant Health Inspection Service, Wildlife Services.

AUTHORS

Richard A. Dolbeer, Science Advisor, Airport Wildlife Hazards Program, USDA, APHIS, Wildlife Services, 6100 Columbus Ave., Sandusky, OH 44870

Sandra E. Wright, Wildlife Strike Database Manager, Airport Wildlife Hazards Program, USDA, APHIS, Wildlife Services, 6100 Columbus Ave., Sandusky, OH 44870

John Weller, National Wildlife Biologist, Office of Airport Safety and Standards, Federal Aviation Administration, 800 Independence Ave., SW, Washington, DC 20591

Michael J. Begier, National Coordinator, Airport Wildlife Hazards Program, USDA, APHIS, Wildlife Services, 1400 Independence Ave., SW, Washington, DC 20250

COVER

Resident Canada geese and white-tailed deer foraging on both sides of a runway at a General Aviation airport in eastern North Carolina represent two of the top three most hazardous species groups involved in wildlife strikes with aircraft. The resident (non-migratory) Canada goose population in North America increased about 4-fold from 1 million in 1990 to 3.9 million in 2008 while white-tailed deer more than doubled in number between 1985 and 2005 from 14 million to over 30 million, respectively.

Anyone with quality photographs of aircraft damage resulting from wildlife strikes or of wildlife at airports is encouraged to submit them to one of the authors for consideration in future wildlife strike publications.

TABLE OF CONTENTS

LIST OF TABLES   iii

LIST OF FIGURES   iv

LIST OF APPENDICES   iv

ACKNOWLEDGMENTS   v

EXECUTIVE SUMMARY   vii

WILDLIFE STRIKES TO CIVIL AIRCRAFT IN THE UNITED STATES, 1990–2008   1

LITERATURE CITED   14

TABLES   19

FIGURES   52

APPENDIX A. SELECTED SIGNIFICANT STRIKES TO CIVIL AIRCRAFT IN THE UNITED STATES, 2008   54

LIST OF TABLES

Table 1.   Number of reported wildlife strikes to civil aircraft by wildlife group, USA, 1990–2008(see Figure 1).   19

Table 2.   Source of information for reported wildlife strikes to civil aircraft, USA, 1990–2008.   20

Table 3.   Person filing report of wildlife strike to civil aircraft, USA, 1990–2008.   21

Table 4.   Number of reported wildlife strikes to civil aircraft by type of operator, USA, 1990–2008.   21

Table 5.   Number of reported bird, bat, terrestrial mammal, and reptile strikes to civil aircraft by USA state, including the District of Columbia (DC), Puerto Rico (PR), USA-possessed Pacific Islands (PI), and the U.S. Virgin Islands (VI), 1990–2008.   22

Table 6.   Number of reported bird and terrestrial mammal strikes to civil aircraft by month, USA, 1990–2008.   23

Table 7.   Reported time of occurrence of wildlife strikes to civil aircraft, USA, 1990–2008.   24

Table 8.   Reported phase of flight at time of wildlife strikes to civil aircraft, USA, 1990–2008.   25

Table 9.   Number of reported bird strikes to civil aircraft by height (feet) above ground level (AGL), USA, 1990–2008.   26

Table 10.   Civil aircraft components reported as being struck and damaged by wildlife, USA, 1990–2008.   27

Table 11.   Number of civil aircraft with reported damage resulting from wildlife strikes, USA, 1990–2008.   28

Table 12   Number of civil aircraft with reported damage resulting from bird and terrestrial mammal strikes by year, USA, 1990–2008.   29

Table 13.   Reported effect-on-flight of wildlife strikes to civil aircraft, USA, 1990–2008.   30

Table 14.   Total reported strikes, strikes causing damage, strikes having a negative effect-on-flight (EOF), strikes involving >1 animal, aircraft downtime, and costs by identified wildlife species for civil aircraft, USA, 1990–2008.   31

Table 15.   Number of reported strikes, strikes with damage, and strikes   47
            having a negative effect-on-flight (EOF) for the four most
            commonly struck bird groups and three most commonly struck
            terrestrial mammal groups, civil aircraft, USA, 1990–2008.

Table 16.   Number of strikes to civil aircraft causing human fatality or injury   48
            and number of injuries and fatalities by wildlife species, USA,
            1990–2008.

Table 17.   Number of civil aircraft lost (destroyed or damaged beyond   49
            repair) after striking wildlife by wildlife species and aircraft mass
            category, USA, 1990-2008.

Table 18.   Number of reported wildlife strikes indicating damage or a   50
            negative effect-on-flight (EOF) and reported losses in hours of
            downtime and U.S. dollars for civil aircraft, USA, 1990–2008.

LIST OF FIGURES

Figure 1.   Number of reported bird (N = 87,416) and terrestrial mammal   52
            (N = 1,912) strikes to civil aircraft, USA, 1990–2008.
            Additionally, 299 and 100 strikes involving bats and reptiles,
            respectively, were reported for a total of 89,727 strikes by all
            species of wildlife (see Table 1).

Figure 2.   Number of reported bird (N = 9,606) and terrestrial mammal (N   52
            = 738) strikes causing damage to civil aircraft, USA, 1990–2008.
            Additionally, 7 and 1 damaging strikes involving bats and
            reptiles, respectively, were reported for a total of 10,352
            damaging strikes by all species of wildlife (see Tables 11, 12).

LIST OF APPENDICES

Appendix A. Selected Significant Strikes To Civil Aircraft In The United   54
            States, 2008

ACKNOWLEDGMENTS

The database files and support programs used to enter and organize strike data initially were established by *E. LeBoeuf* and *J. Rapol*, Federal Aviation Administration (FAA), Office of Airport Safety and Standards, Washington, DC, and were subsequently updated by *A. M. Dickey* and *A. Newman*, Embry-Riddle Aeronautical University, Prescott, Arizona. *E. C. Cleary*, who retired from the FAA in 2007, was instrumental in developing and co-authoring previous reports in this series. We acknowledge his long-standing contributions to the database. We greatly appreciate the assistance provided by these above-acknowledged professionals. *S. Agrawal* and *R. King*, FAA William J. Hughes Technical Center, Atlantic City, NJ also provided critical support and advice. Finally, we acknowledge and thank all of the people who took the time and effort to report wildlife strikes – pilots, mechanics, control tower personnel, airport operations personnel, airline flight safety officers, U.S. Department of Agriculture, Animal and Plant Health Inspection Service, Wildlife Services biologists, and many others. Sponsorship and funds for the ongoing maintenance and analysis of the FAA National Wildlife Strike Database are provided by the FAA, Office of Airport Safety and Standards, Washington, DC, and Airports Division, Airport Technology Branch, FAA William J. Hughes Technical Center, Atlantic City, NJ.

This page intentionally left blank

EXECUTIVE SUMMARY

The 7,516 reported wildlife strikes to U.S. civil aircraft in 2008 brought the 19 year total of wildlife strikes between 1990 and 2008 to 89,727. Birds (97.4%) and terrestrial mammals (2.1%) were struck 72% of the time at or below 500 feet AGL and 92% of the time at or below 3,000 feet AGL. Both classes of animals were struck more often in the late summer/ autumn season. Fifty-one percent of bird strikes occurred between July and October while 61% of terrestrial mammal strikes occurred between July and November. Terrestrial mammals are more likely to be struck at night (64%) whereas birds are struck more often during the day (62%). Both birds (60%) and terrestrial mammals (55%) are more likely to be struck during the landing (i.e., descent, approach or landing roll) phase of flight compared to take-off and climb (37% and 34%, respectively).

During the five years between 2004 and 2008 there was an average of 20 reported wildlife strikes/ day. Although aircraft strikes with terrestrial mammals resulted in a much higher likelihood of damage than strikes with birds (59% to 14%, respectively) the overall likelihood of a strike resulting in damage is 15%. Forty-nine strikes (<1% of total) have resulted in a destroyed aircraft; thirty-three (67%) of these occurred at a General Aviation airport.

Events in early 2009 amplified public awareness of wildlife strikes to aircraft. The dramatic "forced landing" of US Airways Flight 1549 in the Hudson River on 15 January 2009 after Canada geese were ingested in both engines on the Airbus 320 (National Transportation Safety Board 2009, Marra et al. 2009) dramatically demonstrated to the public at large that bird strikes are a serious aviation safety issue.

Historically, this annual report was based on information from a portion of the available data fields contained in the National Wildlife Strike Database (i.e., annual reports from 1994 – current). These reports provided summary information on the nature of wildlife strikes in a format that was found useful by the aviation industry. However, the National Wildlife Strike Database was made available by the FAA to the public on April 24, 2009 and interested parties now have the opportunity to query and examine the data independently. It is important to note that wildlife strike reporting is currently voluntary and un-even. Analyses of the database can produce dissimilar comparisons that involve subject matter such as airports and airlines. Future editions of this annual report will explore additional data summaries that involve all fields contained within the National Wildlife Strike Database.

There continues to be a need for increased and more detailed reporting of information concerning wildlife strikes. Reported strikes have gradually increased each year since 1990 yet only 44% have provided information on the type of bird struck and only 28% of the reports identified the birds to species level.

AP photo

US Airways Flight 1549 in the Hudson River on 15 January 2009

This page intentionally left blank

WILDLIFE STRIKES TO CIVIL AIRCRAFT IN THE UNITED STATES, 1990–2008

A Cessna 500 Citation crashed in a woodlot shortly after take-off from Wiley Post Airport, Oklahoma City, Oklahoma on 4 March 2008. Analysis of organic remains recovered from the aircraft by a U.S. Department of Agriculture (USDA) wildlife biologist under the direction of the National Transportation Safety Board indicated that the aircraft had struck at least 1 American white pelican during the initial climb (Dove et al. 2009). All 5 people on board were killed. Photo by USDA.

INTRODUCTION

This report presents a summary analysis of data from the FAA's National Wildlife Strike Database for the 19-year period 1990 through 2008. Unless noted otherwise, all totals are for the 19-year period, and percentages are of the total known. Because of the large amount of data, most tables do not display data for individual years, 1990 through 2008.

Civil and military aviation communities have long recognized that the threat to human health and safety from aircraft collisions with wildlife (wildlife strikes) is real and increasing (Dolbeer 2000, MacKinnon et al. 2001). Globally, wildlife strikes have killed more than 229 people and destroyed over 210 aircraft since 1988 (Richardson and West 2000; Thorpe 2003; 2005; Dolbeer, unpublished data). Three factors that contribute to this increasing threat are:

1. Many populations of wildlife species commonly involved in strikes have increased markedly in the last few decades and adapted to living in urban environments, including airports. For example, from 1980 to 2007, the resident (non-migratory) Canada goose population in the USA and Canada increased at a mean rate of 7.3 percent per year (Sauer et al. 2008). Other species showing significant mean annual rates of increase included bald eagles (4.6 percent), wild turkeys (12.1 percent), turkey vultures (2.2 percent), American white pelicans (2.9 percent), double-crested cormorants (4.0 percent), and sandhill cranes (5.0 percent). Thirteen of the 14 bird species in North America with mean body masses greater than 8 lbs have shown significant population increases over the past three decades (Dolbeer and Eschenfelder 2003). The white-tailed deer population increased from a low of about 350,000 in 1900 to over 30 million in the past decade (McCabe and McCabe 1997, Hubbard et al. 2000, Adams et al. 2005).

Data from North American Breeding Bird Survey
http://www.mbr-pwrc.usgs.gov/bbs/bbs.html

The American white pelican population in North America increased at a mean annual rate of 4.3 percent from 1966-2007.

2. Concurrent with population increases of many large bird species, air traffic has increased substantially since 1980. Passenger enplanements in the USA increased from about 310 million in 1980 to 750 million in 2008 (3.2 percent per year), and commercial air traffic increased from about 18 million aircraft movements in 1980 to

28 million in 2008 (1.6 percent per year, Federal Aviation Administration 2009). USA commercial air traffic is predicted to continue growing at a rate of about 1.3 percent per year to 35 million movements by 2025.

3. Commercial air carriers have replaced their older three- or four-engine aircraft fleets with more efficient and quieter, two-engine aircraft. In 1965, about 90 percent of the 2,100 USA passenger aircraft had three or four engines. In 2005, the USA passenger fleet had grown to about 8,200 aircraft, and only about 10 percent had three or four engines (U.S. Department of Transportation 2009). With the steady advances in technology over the past several decades, today's two-engine aircraft are more powerful than yesterday's three- and four-engine aircraft, and they are more reliable. However, in the event of a multiple ingestion event (e.g., the US Airways Flight 1549 incident on 15 January 2009), aircraft with two engines may have vulnerabilities not shared by their three or four engine-equipped counterparts. Additionally, previous research has indicated that birds are less able to detect and avoid modern jet aircraft with quieter turbofan engines (Chapter 3, International Civil Aviation Organization 1993) than older aircraft with noisier (Chapter 2) engines (Burger 1983, Kelly et al. 1999).

Whereas 3- or 4-engine aircraft dominated the U.S. passenger fleet 40 years ago, about 90 percent of aircraft today have 2 engines. Populations of large flocking birds are on the increase; in the unlikely event of a multiple ingestion event, aircraft with two engines may have vulnerabilities not shared by their three or four engine-equipped counterparts. In this photo, the propane cannon in the foreground is part of an integrated program to disperse birds from runways at JFK International Airport. Photo by R. Dolbeer.

As a result of these factors, experts within the Federal Aviation Administration (FAA), U.S. Department of Agriculture (USDA), and U.S. Navy and U.S. Air Force expect the risk, frequency, and potential severity of wildlife-aircraft collisions to grow over the next decade.

The FAA has initiated several programs to address this important safety issue. Among the various programs is the collection and analysis of data from wildlife strikes. The FAA began collecting wildlife strike data in 1965. However, except for cursory examinations of the strike reports to determine general trends, the data were never submitted to rigorous analysis until the 1990s. In 1995, the FAA, through an interagency agreement with the USDA, APHIS, Wildlife Services, (USDA/APHIS/WS), initiated a project to obtain more objective estimates of the magnitude and nature of the national wildlife strike problem for civil aviation. This project involves having specialists from the USDA/APHIS/WS: (1) edit all strike reports (FAA Form 5200-7, *Birds/Other Wildlife Strike Report*) received by the FAA since 1990 to ensure consistent, error-free data; (2) enter all edited strike reports in the FAA National Wildlife Strike Database; (3) supplement FAA-reported strikes with additional, non-duplicated strike reports from other sources; (4) provide the FAA with an updated computer file each month containing all edited strike reports; and (5) assist the FAA with the production of annual and special reports summarizing the results of analyses of the data from the National Wildlife Strike Database. Such analyses are critical to determining the economic cost of wildlife strikes, the magnitude of safety issues, and most important, the nature of the problems (e.g., wildlife species involved, types of damage, height and phase of flight during which strikes occur, and seasonal patterns). The information obtained from these analyses provides the foundation for FAA policies and guidance and for refinements in the development, implementation, and justification of integrated research and management efforts to reduce wildlife strikes.

The first annual report on wildlife strikes to civil aircraft in the USA, covering 1994, was completed in November 1995 (Dolbeer et al. 1995). Since then we have published subsequent reports covering the years 1993–1995, 1992–1996, 1991–1997, 1990–1998, 1990–1999, 1990–2000, 1990–2001, 1990-2002, 1990-2003, 1990-2004, 1990-2005, 1990-2006, 1990-2007 (Cleary et al. 1996, 1997, 1998, 1999, 2000, 2002a, 2002b, 2003, 2004, 2005, 2006, 2007; Dolbeer and Wright 2008). This is the 15th report in the series and covers the 19-year period, 1990-2008. All of these annual reports are accessible as PDF documents at http://wildlife-mitigation.tc.faa.gov.

A sample of significant wildlife strikes to civil aircraft in the USA during 2008 is presented in Appendix A. These recent strike examples demonstrate the widespread and diverse nature of the problem. A more extensive list of significant strike events, 1990-2008, is available at http://wildlife-mitigation.tc.faa.gov/public_html/index.html.

RESULTS

NUMBER OF REPORTED STRIKES

For the 19-year period (1990-2008), 89,727 strikes were reported to the FAA. Birds were involved in 97.4 percent of the reported strikes, terrestrial mammals in 2.1 percent, bats in 0.3 percent and reptiles in 0.1 percent (Table 1).

The number of strikes annually reported more than quadrupled from 1,759 in 1990 to 7,516 in 2008 (Table 1, Figure 1). We suggest that the increase in reports from 1990 to 2008 was the result of several factors: an increased awareness of the wildlife strike issue, an increase in aircraft operations, an increase in populations of hazardous wildlife species, and an increase in the number of strikes (Dolbeer 2000, Dolbeer and Eschenfelder 2003).

METHODS OF REPORTING STRIKES

Most (66 percent) of the 89,727 strike reports were filed using the paper (43 percent) or electronic (23 percent) version of FAA Form 5200-7, *Bird/Other Wildlife Strike Report*. Since the online version of this form became available in April 2001, use of the electronic reporting system has climbed dramatically. In 2008, 68 percent of the strike reports were submitted electronically compared to 20 percent in 2002 (Table 2).

SOURCE OF REPORTS

Airline personnel and pilots filed 29 percent and 24 percent of the strike reports, respectively (Table 3). About 85 percent of the reported strikes involved commercial aircraft; the remainder involved business, private, and government aircraft (Table 4).

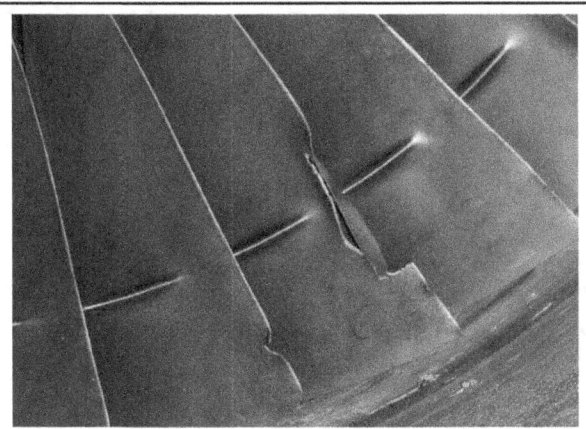 

During approach to a southern USA airport in December 2008, a gadwall was ingested into the #3 engine of an MD-10 at 2,700 feet AGL. The engine and cowling had to be replaced. Time out of service was over 3 days and repair costs exceeded $900,000. Gadwalls (19 incidents) were 1 of 30 species of ducks involved in strikes with civil aircraft in USA, 1990-2008 (Table 14). Engine photo courtesy of Federal Express.

Reports were received from all 50 states, from some USA territories, and from foreign countries when USA-registered aircraft were involved (Table 5). California, Texas, Florida, and New York had the most (7,442, 5,963. 5,571, and 4,732, respectively) bird strike reports. Twenty-one other states each had more than 1,000 bird strikes reported. New York, California, Texas, Colorado, and Illinois each had 100 or more terrestrial mammal strikes. In all, strikes were reported at 1,671 airports (1,456 airports in the USA and 215 foreign airports where USA-based aircraft were involved).

TIMING OF OCCURRENCE OF STRIKES

Most bird strikes (51 percent) occurred between July and October (Table 6); 62 percent occurred during the day (Table 7); 60 percent occurred during the landing (descent, approach, or landing roll) phase of flight; and 37 percent occurred during takeoff and climb (Table 8).

5

This MD-88 struck a yellow-crowned night heron at night at 6,000 feet AGL during descent into a Florida airport, March 2008. Cost of repairs was $17,000.

Most terrestrial mammal strikes (56 percent) occurred between July and November; with 32 percent of deer strikes concentrated in October-November (Table 6). Most terrestrial mammal strikes (64 percent) occurred at night (Table 7), 55 percent occurred during the landing roll, and 34 percent occurred during the takeoff run.

HEIGHT ABOVE GROUND LEVEL (AGL) OF STRIKES

About 59 percent of the bird strikes occurred when the aircraft was at a height of 100 feet or less AGL, 72 percent occurred at 500 feet or less AGL, and 92 percent occurred at or below 3,000 feet AGL (Table 9). Less than 2 percent of bird strikes occurred above 10,000 feet AGL. The record height for a reported bird strike involving civil aircraft in USA was 32,500 feet AGL. Terrestrial mammal strikes predominately occurred at 0 feet AGL; however, 9 percent of the reported strikes occurred while the aircraft was in the air, e.g., when the aircraft struck deer with the landing gear (Table 8).

AIRCRAFT COMPONENTS DAMAGED

The aircraft components most commonly reported as struck by birds were the nose/radome, windshield, engine, wing/rotor, and fuselage (Table 10). Aircraft engines were the component most frequently reported as being damaged by bird strikes (32 percent of all damaged components). There were 11,060 strike events in which a total of 11,616 engines were reported as struck (10,525 events with one engine struck, 518 with two engines struck, 12 with three engines struck, and 5 with four engines struck). In 3,484 damaging bird-strike events involving engines, a total of 3,596 engines was damaged (3,375 events with one engine damaged, 107 with two engines damaged, 1 with three engines damaged, and 1 with four engines damaged).

During landing roll at a major east coast airport at 0830 on 28 April 2008, a Boeing 737 hit a white-tailed deer. The aircraft was taken out of service for inspection and to replace engine cowling. From 1990-2008, 1,920 strikes with terrestrial mammals, including 782 deer strikes, were reported for civil aircraft. Photo by USDA.

Aircraft components most commonly reported as struck by terrestrial mammals were the landing gear, propeller, and wing/rotor. These same components ranked highest for the parts most often reported as damaged by mammals (Table 10).

REPORTED DAMAGE AND EFFECT-ON-FLIGHT

Of the 87,416 bird strikes reported, 68,653 provided some indication as to the nature and extent of any damage. Of these 68,653 reports, 59,047 (86 percent) indicated the strike did not damage the aircraft; 5,112 (7 percent) indicated the aircraft suffered minor damage; 2,456 (4 percent) indicated the aircraft suffered substantial damage; 2,015 (3 percent) reported an uncertain level of damage; and 24 reports (less than 1 percent) indicated the aircraft was destroyed as a result of the strike (Table 11).

Of the 1,912 terrestrial mammal strikes reported, 1,246 reports provided some indication as to the nature and extent of any damage. Of these 1,246 reports, 508 (41 percent) indicated the strike did not damage the aircraft; 324 (26 percent) indicated the aircraft suffered minor damage; 331 (27 percent) indicated the aircraft suffered substantial damage; 58 (5 percent) reported an uncertain level of damage; and 25 (2 percent) indicated the aircraft was destroyed as a result of the strike (Table 11). Not surprisingly, a much higher percentage of terrestrial mammal strikes (59 percent) resulted in aircraft damage than did bird strikes (14 percent). Deer (782 strikes, Table 6) were involved in 41 percent of the 1,912 terrestrial mammal strikes.

The number of reported bird strikes with damage to aircraft increased from 327 in 1990 to a peak of 705 in 2000 (Table 12, Figure 2). The number of reported strikes with damage has subsequently declined by 31 percent to 493 in 2008. The number of reported terrestrial mammal strikes with damage has followed a pattern similar to birds. The peak number (58) in 1997 declined to 19 in 2008.

In 12 percent and 52 percent of the bird and terrestrial mammal strike reports, respectively, an adverse effect-on-flight was reported (Table 13). Three percent of bird strikes resulted in an aborted takeoff compared to 17 percent of terrestrial mammal strikes.

(Source U.S. Fish and Wildlife Service)

The resident (non-migratory) Canada goose population in North America increased about 4-fold from 1 million in 1990 to 3.9 million in 2008 (Dolbeer and Seubert 2009). From 1990-2008, 1,181 strikes involving Canada geese and 420 strikes with unidentified or other species of geese were reported for civil aircraft in USA. From 1990-2008, 381 identified species of birds have been struck; 176 species caused aircraft damage.

WILDLIFE SPECIES INVOLVED IN STRIKES

Table 14 shows the number of reported strikes, strikes causing damage, strikes having a negative effect-on-flight, strikes involving >1 animal, the reported aircraft down time, and the reported costs by identified wildlife species for the 19-year period, 1990 through 2008.

Only 38,474 (44 percent) of the 87,416 bird strike reports provided information on the type of bird (e.g., gull or hawk). Furthermore, only 24,351 (63 percent) of these 38,474 reports provided identification to species level (e.g., ring-billed gull or red-tailed hawk; Table 14). Thus, birds were identified to species level in only 28 percent of the 87,416 reported bird strikes. In all, 381 identified species of birds were struck; 176 identified species were reported as causing damage.

Gulls (19 percent), doves/pigeons (15 percent), raptors (13 percent), and waterfowl (8 percent) were the most frequently struck bird groups (Table 15). Gulls were involved in 2.4 times more strikes than waterfowl (7,470 and 3,175, respectively). Waterfowl, however, were involved in 1.2 times more damaging strikes (1,418 or 31 percent of all damaging strikes in which the bird type was identified) than were gulls (1,169 or 25 percent of all damaging strikes in which the bird type was identified). Gulls were responsible for the greatest number of bird strikes (935 or 27 percent) that had a negative effect-on-flight.

The most frequently struck terrestrial mammals were Artiodactyls – primarily deer (43 percent) – and Carnivores – primarily coyotes (34 percent) (Tables 14, 15). Artiodactyls were responsible for 92 percent of the mammal strikes that resulted in damage and 79 percent of the mammal strikes that had a negative effect-on-flight. In all, 33 identified species of terrestrial mammals and 8 identified species of bats were reported struck; 19 identified species of terrestrial mammals and 1 identified species of bat caused damage (Table 14).

HUMAN FATALITIES AND INJURIES DUE TO WILDLIFE STRIKES

For the 19-year period, reports were received of 9 wildlife strikes that resulted in 16 human fatalities (Table 16). Five of these strikes resulting in 7 fatalities involved unidentified species of birds. American white pelicans, Canada geese, white-tailed deer and brown-pelicans were responsible for the other 9 fatalities. Reports were received of 167 strikes that resulted in 209 human injuries. Waterfowl (ducks and geese; 40 strikes, 45 humans injured), vultures (24 strikes, 26 injuries), and deer (18 strikes, 25 injuries) caused 82 (62 percent) of the 132 strikes resulting in injuries in which the species or species group was identified (Table 16).

AIRCRAFT DESTROYED DUE TO WILDLIFE STRIKES

For the 19-year period, reports were received of 49 aircraft destroyed or damaged beyond repair due to wildlife strikes (Tables 11, 12, 17). The majority (63 percent) were small ($\leq$2,250 kg maximum takeoff mass) general aviation (GA) aircraft. Terrestrial mammals (primarily white-tailed deer) were responsible for 25 (51 percent) of the incidents. Canada geese (4 incidents) and vultures (3 incidents) were responsible for 7 (60 percent) of the 14 incidents involving birds in which the species or species group was identified.

This Piper 28 aircraft was damaged beyond repair after striking a white-tailed deer on landing roll at a General Aviation airport in the northeastern USA, September 2008. This was 1 of 6 U.S. civil aircraft destroyed in 2008 after striking wildlife.

Thirty-three (67 percent) of the 49 wildlife strikes resulting in a destroyed aircraft occurred at General Aviation (GA) airports, 9 occurred away from an airport, 6 occurred at USA airports certificated for passenger service under 14 CFR Part 139, and 1 occurred at a foreign airport certificated for passenger service (Table 17). GA airports, often located in rural areas with inadequate fencing to exclude large mammals, face unique challenges in mitigating wildlife risks to aviation (DeVault et al. 2008; Dolbeer et al. 2008).

ECONOMIC LOSSES DUE TO WILDLIFE STRIKES

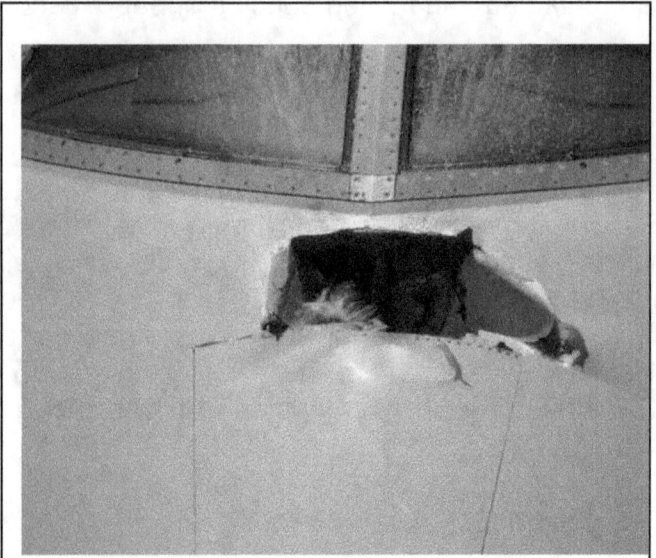

A Challenger 600 struck several American white pelicans at 3,000 feet AGL during climb from a Colorado airport, April 2008. One bird penetrated the nose of aircraft and entered the cockpit. Both engines ingested birds and 1 engine lost power. Pilot was able to return and land safely. Repair costs exceeded $2 million.

For the 19-year period, reported losses from bird strikes totaled 393,521 hours of aircraft downtime and $308.3 million in monetary losses. Reported losses from terrestrial mammal strikes totaled 244,068 hours of aircraft downtime and $38.8 million in monetary losses. Bat strikes resulted in 100 hours of aircraft downtime and $3.2 million in losses. Reptile strikes resulted in 3 hours of aircraft downtime (Table 14).

Of the 15,179 reports that indicated the strike had an adverse effect on the aircraft and/or flight, 4,301 provided an estimate of the aircraft down time (Σ = 637,692 hours, avg. = 148.3 hours down time/incident, Table 18). Of the reports providing a damage cost estimate for the incident; 2,620 gave an estimate of the direct aircraft damage cost (Σ = $308.6 million, avg. = $117,787 damage/incident), and 1,157 gave an estimate of other monetary losses (Σ = $41.7 million, avg. = $36,003 lost/incident). Other monetary losses include such expenses as lost revenue, the cost of putting passengers in hotels, re-scheduling aircraft, and flight cancellations.

Analysis of 14 groups of strike reports from 3 USA airports and 3 airlines for the years 1991-2004 indicated that about 20 percent of all strikes were reported to the FAA (Cleary et al. 2005, Wright and Dolbeer 2005). Additionally, only 28 percent of the 15,179 reports from 1990-2008 indicating an adverse effect provided estimates of aircraft downtime, 17 percent provided estimates of direct costs, and 8 percent provided estimates of other (indirect) costs (Table 18). Furthermore, many reports providing cost estimates were filed before aircraft damage and downtime had been fully assessed. As a result, the information on the number of strikes and associated costs compiled from the voluntary reporting program (summarized by species of wildlife struck in Table 14) is believed to severely underestimate the magnitude of the problem.

Assuming (1) all 15,179 reported wildlife strikes that had an adverse effect on the aircraft and/or flight engendered similar amounts of downtime and/or monetary losses and (2) that these reports are all of the damaging strikes that occurred, then at a minimum, wildlife strikes cost the USA civil aviation industry 118,448 hours per year of aircraft downtime and $123 million in monetary losses ($94 million per year in direct costs and $29 million per year in associated costs, Table 18).

A biologist attaches vinyl strips to the top of a culvert that runs under a runway at a U.S. Air Force base in Oklahoma, 2008. The strips deter swallows from entering the culvert to build nests on the walls. Photo by USDA.

Further, assuming a 20 percent reporting rate, the annual cost of wildlife strikes to the USA civil aviation industry is estimated to be 592,000 hours of aircraft downtime and $614 million in monetary losses ($470 million per year in direct costs and $144 million per year in associated costs, Table 18).

CONCLUSIONS

An analysis of 19 years of strike data reveals the magnitude and severity of the wildlife-aircraft strike problem for civil aviation in the USA. Wildlife strikes continue to pose a significant economic and safety risk for civil aviation in the USA. Management actions to reduce wildlife strikes are being implemented at many airports (e.g., Wenning et al. 2004, DeFusco et al. 2005, Dolbeer 2006a, Human Wildlife Conflicts Journal 2009), and these efforts may be responsible, at least in part, for the general decline in reported strikes with damage from 2000-2008 (Figure 2). For example, USDA/APHIS/WS biologists provided assistance at 764 airports nationwide in 2008 to mitigate wildlife risks to aviation compared to only 42 airports in 1991 and 193 in 1998 (Begier and Dolbeer 2009). However, much work remains to be done to reduce wildlife strikes.

To address the problem, airport managers first need to assess the wildlife hazards on their airports with the help of qualified airport biologists (FAA Advisory Circular 150/5200-36). They then must take appropriate actions, under the guidance of professional biologists trained in wildlife damage management at airports, to minimize the risks posed by wildlife. The aviation community must also widen its view of wildlife management to consider habitats and land uses in proximity to the airport. Wetlands, dredge-spoil containment areas, waste-disposal facilities, and wildlife refuges can attract hazardous wildlife. Such land uses, as discussed in FAA Advisory Circular 150/5200-33b, are often incompatible with aviation safety and should either be prohibited near airports or designed and operated in a manner that minimizes the attraction of hazardous wildlife.

The manual *Wildlife Hazard Management at Airports* (Cleary and Dolbeer 2005) provides guidance to airport personnel and biologists for conducting wildlife hazard assessments and in developing and implementing wildlife hazard management plans. Adobe Acrobat© PDF versions of the manual are available online in English, Spanish, and French at http://wildlife-mitigation.tc.faa.gov.

Finally, there is a need for increased and more detailed reporting of wildlife strikes. Previous analyses (Cleary et al. 2005, Wright and Dolbeer 2005) indicated less than 20 percent of all wildlife strikes involving USA civil aircraft were reported; new information indicates that approximately 39% of wildlife strikes are now reported (Dolbeer unpublished data 2009). Although the quantity of strike reporting is higher more detail is needed. Approximately, 44 percent of all reported bird strikes for 1990-2008, provided information on the type of bird struck, and only about 28 percent of the reports identified the birds struck to species level. In addition, only 17 percent of strike reports indicating an adverse effect on the aircraft or flight provided at least a partial estimate of economic losses resulting from the strike. Increased levels of reporting are positive; however, these types of detailed information can be used to more effectively mitigate wildlife hazards to aviation at the nation's airports.

REPORTING A STRIKE AND IDENTIFYING SPECIES OF WILDLIFE STRUCK

Pilots, airport operations, aircraft maintenance personnel, and anyone else having knowledge of a strike should report the incident to the FAA using FAA Form 5200-7. Strikes can be reported electronically via the internet (http://wildlife-mitigation.tc.faa.gov) or Form 5200-7 can be accessed and printed for mailing in reports.

It is important to include as much information as possible on FAA Form 5200-7. All reports are carefully screened to identify duplicate reports prior to being entered into the database. Reports of the same incident filed by different people are combined and often provide a more complete record of the strike event than would be possible if just one report were filed.

The identification of the exact species of wildlife struck (e.g., ring-billed gull, Canada goose, mallard, mourning dove, or red-tailed hawk as opposed to gull, goose, duck, dove, or hawk) is particularly important. This species information is critical for biologists developing and implementing wildlife risk management programs at airports because a problem that cannot be measured or defined cannot be solved. Bird strike remains that cannot be identified by airport personnel can often be identified by a local biologist trained in ornithology or by sending feather and other remains in a sealed plastic bag (with FAA Form 5200-7) to:

Material sent via Express Mail Service:	Material sent via U.S. Postal Service:
Feather Identification Lab	Feather Identification Lab
Smithsonian Institution NMNH	Smithsonian Institution, NMNH
E600, MRC 116	E600, MRC 116
10th & Constitution Ave. NW	P.O. Box 37012
Washington, D.C. 20560-0116	Washington, D.C. 20013-7012
(label package "safety investigation material")	(not recommended for priority cases)
Phone #s 202-633-0787 or 202-633-0791	

Please send whole feathers whenever possible as diagnostic characteristics are often found in the downy barbules at the feather base. Wings, as well as breast and tail feathers should be sent whenever possible. Beaks, feet, bones, and talons are also useful diagnostic materials. Even blood smears can provide material for DNA analysis (Dove et al. 2008). Do not send entire bird carcasses through the mail. However, photographs of the carcasses can be very useful supplemental documentation.

Additional information on sending bird remains to the Smithsonian is available at: http://wildlife-mitigation.tc.faa.gov.

Scientists at the Smithsonian Feather Lab identify bird species involved in strikes by various techniques, depending on the amount and type of remains recovered. In this photo, whole feather characters are compared with museum specimens. In other situations, microscope slides are made of minute, fragmented material to look for diagnostic characters found in the downy barbules at the base of feathers. Also, mitochondrial DNA can often be extracted from organic remains and compared with species profiles in the Barcode of Life Database (Dove et al. 2008). Finally, photos of the carcass and information on the location, season, and time of day when the strike occurred can be useful in identification. Photo courtesy of Smithsonian Institution.

LITERATURE CITED

Adams, K., J. Hamilton and M. Ross. 2009. Quality Deer Management Association Whitetail Report 2009. 68 pages.

Begier, M. J., and R. A. Dolbeer. 2009. Protecting the flying public and minimizing economic losses within the aviation industry: technical, operational, and research assistance provided by USDA-APHIS-Wildlife Services to reduce wildlife hazards to aviation, Fiscal year 2008. Special report, U.S. Department of Agriculture, Animal and Plant Health Inspection Service, Wildlife Services. Washington D.C. USA. 13 pages.

Burger, J. 1983. Jet aircraft noise and bird strikes: why more birds are being hit. Environmental Pollution (Series A) 30:143–152.

Cleary, E. C., and R. A. Dolbeer. 2005. Wildlife hazard management at airports, a manual for airport operators. Second edition. Federal Aviation Administration, Office of Airport Safety and Standards, Washington, D.C. USA. 348 pages. (http://wildlife-mitigation.tc.faa.gov).

Cleary, E. C., S. E. Wright, and R. A. Dolbeer. 1996. Wildlife strikes to civilian aircraft in the United States, 1993–1995. Serial Report Number 2. DOT/FAA/AAS/97-1. Federal Aviation Administration, Office of Airport Safety and Standards, Washington, D.C. USA. 33 pages.

Cleary, E. C., S. E. Wright, and R. A. Dolbeer. 1997. Wildlife strikes to civil aircraft in the United States, 1992–1996. Serial Report Number 3. DOT/FAA/AAS/97-3. Federal Aviation Administration, Office of Airport Safety and Standards, Washington, D.C. USA. 30 pages.

Cleary, E. C., S. E. Wright, and R. A. Dolbeer. 1998. Wildlife strikes to civil aircraft in the United States, 1991–1997. Serial Report Number 4. Federal Aviation Administration, Office of Airport Safety and Standards, Washington, D.C. USA. 34 pages.

Cleary, E. C., S. E. Wright, and R. A. Dolbeer. 1999. Wildlife strikes to civil aircraft in the United States, 1990–1998. Serial Report Number 5. Federal Aviation Administration, Office of Airport Safety and Standards, Washington, D.C. USA. 33 pages.

Cleary, E. C., S. E. Wright, and R. A. Dolbeer. 2000. Wildlife strikes to civil aircraft in the United States, 1990–1999. Serial Report Number 6. Federal Aviation Administration, Office of Airport Safety and Standards, Washington, D.C. USA. 61 pages.

Cleary, E. C., S. E. Wright, and R. A. Dolbeer. 2002a. Wildlife strikes to civil aircraft in the United States, 1990–2000. Serial Report Number 7. Federal Aviation Administration, Office of Airport Safety and Standards, Washington, D.C. USA. 37 pages.

Cleary, E. C., R. A. Dolbeer, and S. E. Wright. 2002b. Wildlife strikes to civil aircraft in the United States, 1990–2001. U.S. Department of Transportation, Federal Aviation Administration, Serial Report No. 8, DOT/FAA/AS/00-6(AAS-310). Washington D.C. USA. 50 pages.

Cleary, E. C., R. A. Dolbeer, and S. E. Wright. 2003. Wildlife strikes to civil aircraft in the United States, 1990–2002. U.S. Department of Transportation, Federal Aviation Administration, Serial Report No. 9 DOT/FAA/AS/00-6(AAS-310). Washington D.C. USA. 51 pages.

Cleary, E. C., R. A. Dolbeer, and S. E. Wright. 2004. Wildlife strikes to civil aircraft in the United States, 1990–2003. U.S. Department of Transportation, Federal Aviation Administration, Serial Report No. 10 DOT/FAA/AS/00-6(AAS-310). Washington D.C. USA. 54 pages.

Cleary, E. C., R. A. Dolbeer, and S. E. Wright. 2005. Wildlife strikes to civil aircraft in the United States, 1990–2004. U.S. Department of Transportation, Federal Aviation Administration, Serial Report No. 11 DOT/FAA/AS/00-6(AAS-310). Washington D.C. USA. 53 pages.

Cleary, E. C., R. A. Dolbeer, and S. E. Wright. 2006. Wildlife strikes to civil aircraft in the United States, 1990–2005. U.S. Department of Transportation, Federal Aviation Administration, Serial Report No. 12 DOT/FAA/AS/00-6(AAS-310). Washington D.C. USA. 64 pages.

Cleary, E. C., R. A. Dolbeer, and S. E. Wright. 2007. Wildlife strikes to civil aircraft in the United States, 1990–2006. U.S. Department of Transportation, Federal Aviation Administration, Serial Report No. 13 DOT/FAA/AS/00-6(AAS-310). Washington D.C. USA. 59 pages.

DeFusco, R. P., M. J. Hovan, J. T. Harper, and K. A. Heppard. 2005. North American Bird Strike Advisory System, Strategic Plan. Institute for Information Technology Applications, U.S. Air Force Academy, Colorado Springs, Colorado USA. 31 pages.

DeVault, T. L., J. E. Kubel, D. J. Glista, and O. E. Rhodes, Jr. 2008. Mammalian hazards at small airports in Indiana: impact of perimeter fencing. Human-Wildlife Conflicts 2(2):240-247.

Dolbeer, R. A. 2000. Birds and aircraft: fighting for airspace in crowded skies. Pages 37-43 *in* Proceedings of 19th Vertebrate Pest Conference, University of California, Davis, California, USA.

Dolbeer, R. A. 2006*a*. Birds and aircraft compete for space in crowded skies. ICAO Journal 61(3):21-24. International Civil Aviation Organization. Montreal, Canada.

Dolbeer, R. A. 2006*b*. Height distribution of birds recorded by collisions with aircraft. Journal of Wildlife Management 70 (5): 1345-1350.

Dolbeer, R. A., S. E. Wright, and P. Eschenfelder. 2005. Animal ambush at the airport: the need to broaden ICAO standards for bird strikes to include terrestrial wildlife. Pages 102-113 *in* Proceedings of the 27th International Bird Strike Committee meeting (Volume 1). Athens, Greece.

Dolbeer, R. A., M. J. Begier, and S. E. Wright. 2008. Animal ambush: the challenge of managing wildlife hazards at general aviation airports. Proceedings of the 53rd Annual Corporate Aviation Safety Seminar, 30 April-1 May 2008, Palm Harbor, Florida. Flight Safety Foundation, Alexandria, Virginia, USA.

Dolbeer, R. A. and P. Eschenfelder. 2003. Amplified bird-strike risks related to population increases of large birds in North America. Pages 49-67 *in* Proceedings of the 26th International Bird Strike Committee meeting (Volume 1). Warsaw, Poland.

Dolbeer R. A., and J. L. Seubert. 2009. Canada goose populations and strikes with civil aircraft, 1990-2008: challenging trends for aviation industry. Special report, U.S. Department of Agriculture, Wildlife Services, Airport Wildlife Hazards Program, Washington, D.C., March 2009.

Dolbeer, R. A., and S. E. Wright. 2008. Wildlife strikes to civil aircraft in the United States, 1990–2007. U.S. Department of Transportation, Federal Aviation Administration, Serial Report No. 14 DOT/FAA/AS/00-6(AAS-310). Washington D.C. USA. 57 pages.

Dolbeer, R. A., S. E. Wright, and E. C. Cleary. 1995. Bird and other wildlife strikes to civilian aircraft in the United States, 1994. Interim report, DTFA01-91-Z-02004. U.S. Department of Agriculture, for Federal Aviation Administration, FAA Technical Center, Atlantic City, New Jersey, USA. 38 pages.

Dolbeer, R. A., S. E. Wright, and E. C. Cleary. 2000. Ranking the hazard level of wildlife species to aviation. Wildlife Society Bulletin 28:372–378.

Dove C. J., N. Rotzel, M. Heacker, and L. A. Weigt. 2008. Using DNA barcodes to identify bird species involved in birdstrikes. Journal of Wildlife Management 72:1231–1236.

Dove C. J., N. F. Dahlan, and M. Heacker. 2009. Forensic birdstrike identification techniques used in an accident investigation at Wiley Post Airport, Oklahoma, 2008. Human Wildlife Conflicts 3(2): 179–185.

Federal Aviation Administration. 2009. Terminal area forecast (TAF) system. Federal Aviation Administration. Washington, D.C. USA. (http://aspm.faa.gov/main/taf.asp).

Hubbard, M. W., B. J. Danielson, and R. A. Schmitz. 2000. Factors influencing the location of deer-vehicle accidents in Iowa. Journal of Wildlife Management 64:707-713.

Human Wildlife Conflicts Journal. 2009. Special edition on bird strikes. Volume 3, Issue 2. Berryman Institute, Utah State University, Logan Utah USA (http://www.berrymaninstitute.org).

International Civil Aviation Organization. 1989. Manual on the ICAO Bird Strike Information System (IBIS). Third Edition. Montreal, Quebec, Canada.

International Civil Aviation Organization. 1993. Convention on international civil aviation (international standards and recommended practices). Annex 16: Environmental Protection. Third edition. Montreal, Quebec, Canada.

Kelly, T. C., R. Bolger, and M. J. A. O'Callaghan. 1999. The behavioral response of birds to commercial aircraft. Pages 77-82 in Bird Strike '99, Proceedings of Bird Strike Committee-USA/Canada Meeting. Vancouver, B.C., Canada: Transport Canada, Ottawa, Ontario, Canada.

MacKinnon, B., R. Sowden, and S. Dudley, (editors). 2001. Sharing the skies: an aviation guide to the management of wildlife hazards. Transport Canada, Aviation Publishing Division, AARA, 5th Floor, Tower C, 330 Sparks Street, Ottawa, Ontario, K1A 0N8, Canada. 316 pages.

Marra, P. P., C. J. Dove, R. A. Dolbeer, N. F. Dahlan, M. Heacker, J. F. Whatton, N. E. Diggs, C. France, and G. A. Henkes. 2009. Migratory Canada geese cause crash of US Airways Flight 1549. Frontiers in Ecology and the Environment. 7(6): 297-301.

McCabe, T. R., and R. E. McCabe. 1997. Recounting whitetails past. Pages 11–26 in W. J. McShea, H. B. Underwood, and J. H. Rappole (editors). The science of overabundance: deer ecology and population management. Smithsonian Institution. Washington D.C. USA. 402 pages.

National Transportation Safety Board. 2009. Fourth update on investigation into ditching of US Airways jetliner into Hudson River. NTSB Advisory, 12 February 2009. National Transportation Safety Board, Washington, DC USA. (http://www.ntsb.gov/Pressrel/2009/090212b.html).

Richardson, W. J., and T. West. 2000. Serious birdstrike accidents to military aircraft: updated list and summary. Pages 67–98 in Proceedings of 25th International Bird Strike Committee Meeting. Amsterdam, Netherlands.

Sauer, J. R., J. E. Hines, and J. Fallon. 2008. The North American Breeding Bird Survey, results and analysis 1966 - 2007. Version 5.15.2008. U.S. Geological Survey, Patuxent Wildlife Research Center, Laurel, Maryland, USA. (http://www.mbr-pwrc.usgs.gov/bbs/bbs.html).

Thorpe, J. 2003. Fatalities and destroyed aircraft due to bird strikes, 1912–2002. Pages 85–113 *in* Proceedings of the 26th International Bird Strike Committee Meeting (Volume 1). Warsaw, Poland.

Thorpe, J. 2005. Fatalities and destroyed aircraft due to bird strikes, 2002-2004 (with an appendix of animal strikes). Pages 17-24 *in* Proceedings of the 27th International Bird Strike Committee Meeting (Volume 1). Athens, Greece.

U.S. Department of Transportation. 2009. National Transportation Statistics. Table 1-13: Active U.S. Air Carrier and General Aviation Fleet by Type of Aircraft Research and Innovative Technology Administration.. Washington D.C. USA). http://www.bts.gov/publications/national_transportation_statistics/html/table_01_13.html

Wenning, K. M., M. J. Begier, and R. A. Dolbeer. 2004. Wildlife hazard management at airports: fifteen years of growth and progress for Wildlife Services. Pages 295-301 *in* Proceedings of 21st Vertebrate Pest Conference, University of California, Davis, California, USA.

Wright, S. E. and R. A. Dolbeer. 2005. Percentage of wildlife strikes reported and species identified under a voluntary system. *in* Proceedings of Bird Strike Committee USA/Canada meeting, Vancouver, B.C. Canada (http://www.birdstrikecanada.com).

TABLES

Table 1. Number of reported wildlife strikes to civil aircraft by wildlife group, USA, 1990–2008 (see Figure 1)[1].

	Number of reported strikes-all aircraft					Commercial aircraft only[1]		
Year	Birds	Bats	Terrestrial mammals[2]	Reptiles[2]	Total	Total	Movements (x 1 million)[3]	Strikes/ 10,000 movements
1990	1,738	4	17	0	1,759	1,322	23.29	0.568
1991	2,252	3	36	0	2,291	1,769	24.80	0.713
1992	2,351	2	56	1	2,410	1,800	25.20	0.714
1993	2,395	6	53	0	2,454	1,779	25.59	0.695
1994	2,459	2	73	1	2,535	1,905	26.61	0.716
1995	2,643	5	69	8	2,725	2,019	27.07	0.746
1996	2,840	1	91	3	2,935	2,087	27.60	0.756
1997	3,351	1	92	14	3,458	2,457	27.79	0.884
1998	3,656	3	105	7	3,771	2,521	28.03	0.899
1999	5,001	7	89	1	5,098	3,849	28.77	1.338
2000	5,873	16	120	3	6,012	4,482	29.56	1.516
2001	5,647	8	137	8	5,801	4,164	29.17	1.427
2002	6,047	19	116	15	6,197	4,406	27.64	1.594
2003	5,853	20	124	5	6,003	4,283	27.92	1.534
2004	6,399	27	118	6	6,550	4,685	28.90	1.621
2005	7,076	27	130	7	7,240	5,170	29.26	1.767
2006	7,042	49	140	9	7,240	4,915	28.32	1.736
2007	7,507	53	167	7	7,734	4,998	28.48	1.755
2008	7,286	46	179	5	7,516	4,543	27.93	1.626
Total	**87,416**	**299**	**1,912**	**100**	**89,727**	**63,154**	**521.91**	**1.210**

[1] See Table 4.

[2] For terrestrial mammals and reptiles, species with body masses <1 kilogram (2.2 lbs) are excluded from database (Dolbeer et al. 2005).

[3] Departures and arrivals by air carrier, commuter, and air taxi service (Federal Aviation Administration 2009).

Table 2. Source of information for reported wildlife strikes to civil aircraft, USA, 1990–2008.

Source	19-year total	% of total known
FAA Form 5200-7[1] (Paper)	38,910	43
FAA Form 5200-7E[2] (Electronic)	20,910	23
Airline report	13,120	15
Multiple[3]	7,703	9
Airport report	4,413	5
Other[4]	1,184	1
Preliminary Aircraft Incident Report	888	1
Engine manufacturer	830	1
Aircraft Incident Report	780	1
Daily report (FAA)	659	1
Aviation Safety Reporting System	183	0
National Transportation Safety Board	78	0
Aircraft Incident Preliminary Notice	69	0
Total	**89,727**	**100**

[1] Bird/Other Wildlife Strike Report

[2] Electronic filing of reports (http://wildlife-mitigation.tc.faa.gov) began in April 2001. In 2001, 0.4 percent of reports were filed electronically compared to 20, 28, 32, 37, 46, 62, and 68 percent in 2002-2008, respectively.

[3] More than one type of report was filed for the same strike.

[4] Various sources, such as news media and Commercial Incident Reports.

Table 3. Person filing report of wildlife strike to civil aircraft, USA, 1990–2008.

Person filing report	19-year total	% of total known
Airline Operations	21,285	29
Pilot	17,364	24
Carcass Found[1]	14,220	20
Tower	9,126	13
Airport Operations	8,546	12
Other	1,969	3
Total known	**72,510**	**100**
Unknown	**17,217**	
Total	**89,727**	

[1] Airport personnel found wildlife remains within 200 feet of a runway centerline that appeared to have been struck by aircraft and no strike was reported by pilot, tower, or airline.

Table 4. Number of reported wildlife strikes to civil aircraft by type of operator, USA, 1990–2008.

Type of operator	19-year total	% of total known
Commercial	63,154	85
Business	8,339	11
Private	1,984	3
Government/Police[1]	442	1
Total known	**73,919**	**100**
Unknown	**15,808**	
Total	**89,727**	

[1] U.S. Coast Guard aircraft were involved in 144 of these strikes.

Table 5. Number of reported bird, bat, terrestrial mammal, and reptile strikes to civil aircraft by USA state, including the District of Columbia (DC), Puerto Rico (PR), USA-possessed Pacific Islands (PI), and the U.S. Virgin Islands (VI), 1990–2008.

State	Reported strikes (19-year total)					State	Reported strikes (19-year total)				
	Birds	Bats	T. mam-mals	Rep-tiles	Total		Birds	Bats	T. mam-mals	Rep-tiles	Total
AK	621	1	29	0	651	NC	1,445	2	30	0	1,477
AL	683	2	11	0	696	ND	286	0	14	0	300
AR	323	1	15	0	339	NE	936	7	16	0	959
AZ	1,377	32	63	0	1,472	NH	468	7	7	0	482
CA	7,442	3	112	0	7,557	NJ	2,389	3	92	11	2,495
CO	2,836	9	106	0	2,951	NM	220	0	27	0	247
CT	906	1	20	0	927	NV	438	0	8	0	446
DC	1,946	4	43	0	1,993	NY	4,732	8	142	23	4,905
DE	67	0	1	0	68	OH	2,894	8	85	0	2,987
FL	5,571	9	72	48	5,700	OK	804	1	30	5	840
GA	1,326	2	32	0	1,360	OR	1,481	2	9	0	1,492
HI	1,982	0	8	0	1,990	PA	2,769	4	80	0	2,853
IA	646	2	19	0	667	PI	156	0	0	0	156
ID	228	0	8	0	236	PR	151	2	0	5	158
IL	3,958	5	100	1	4,064	RI	366	1	13	0	380
IN	1,128	2	24	0	1,154	SC	394	0	19	0	413
KS	263	1	7	0	271	SD	176	0	13	1	190
KY	2,222	4	17	0	2,243	TN	2,591	2	20	0	2,613
LA	1,446	5	20	2	1,473	TX	5,963	88	108	1	6,160
MA	1,149	1	24	0	1,174	UT	1,109	3	19	0	1,131
MD	962	6	62	0	1,030	VA	1,086	3	59	0	1,148
ME	262	0	12	0	274	VI	95	0	0	0	95
MI	2,128	11	85	1	2,225	VT	101	0	3	0	104
MN	869	10	24	0	903	WA	1,341	2	18	0	1,361
MO	1,979	9	35	0	2,023	WI	788	3	53	0	844
MS	274	0	9	0	283	WV	187	0	50	0	237
MT	129	0	9	0	138	WY	78	0	6	0	84
						Total known[1]	76,167	266	1,888	98	78,419
						Foreign[2]	1,828	10	9	0	1,847
						Unknown	9,421	23	15	2	9,461
						Total	87,416	299	1,912	100	89,727

[1] Strikes were reported at 1,456 airports in the USA.

[2] Strikes to USA air carriers were reported at 215 foreign airports.

Table 6. Number of reported bird and terrestrial mammal strikes to civil aircraft by month, USA, 1990–2008[1].

Month	All birds		All terrestrial mammals		Deer only[2]	
	19-year total	% of total known	19-year total	% of total known	19-year total	% of total known
Jan	3,289	4	108	6	39	5
Feb	2,931	3	89	5	33	4
Mar	4,639	5	123	6	40	5
Apr	6,202	7	117	6	45	6
May	8,322	10	109	6	34	4
Jun	6,651	8	164	9	54	7
Jul	10,107	12	199	10	70	9
Aug	11,767	13	226	12	81	10
Sep	11,753	13	196	10	78	10
Oct	11,118	13	236	12	102	13
Nov	6,621	8	238	12	151	19
Dec	4,016	5	107	6	55	7
Total	**87,416**	**100**	**1,912**	**100**	**782**	**100**

[1] In addition, 299 strikes with bats were reported of which 55 percent occurred in July - September; 100 strikes with reptiles were reported of which 64 percent occurred in May - August.

[2] Deer strikes were comprised of 729 white-tailed deer, 37 mule deer, and 16 deer not identified to species. Other wild artiodactyls struck (but not included in this column of table) were 9 wapiti (elk), 7 pronghorns, 4 moose, 2 caribou, 1 swine (feral hog) and 2 collared peccaries (Table 14).

Table 7. Reported time of occurrence of wildlife strikes to civil aircraft, USA, 1990–2008[1].

Time of day	Birds		Terrestrial mammals	
	19-year total	% of total known	19-year total	% of total known
Dawn	2,422	4	38	3
Day	35,633	62	277	23
Dusk	3,010	5	111	9
Night	16,449	29	757	64
Total known	**57,514**	**100**	**1,183**	**100**
Unknown	**29,902**		**729**	
Total[1]	**87,416**		**1,912**	

[1] In addition, 299 strikes with bats were reported: time not reported (224), night (58), dusk (6), day (9), and dawn (2). Also, 100 strikes with reptiles were reported: time not reported (83), day (10), night (4), dusk (2), and dawn (1).

Table 8. Reported phase of flight at time of wildlife strikes to civil aircraft, USA, 1990–2008[1].

Phase of flight	Birds		Terrestrial mammals	
	19-year total	% of total known	19-year total	% of total known
Parked	33	<1	1	<1
Taxi	244	<1	32	2
Takeoff run	12,289	19	450	34
Climb	11,547	18	29	2
En route	1,532	2	0	0
Descent	2,422	4	0	0
Approach	24,941	39	88	7
Landing roll	10,538	17	721	55
Total known	**63,546**	**100**	**1,321**	**100**
Unknown	**23,870**		**591**	
Total[1]	**87,416**		**1,912**	

[1] In addition, 299 strikes with bats were reported: phase of flight not reported (226), approach (45), climb (8), descent (5), landing roll (10), en route (2), and takeoff run (3). Also, 99 strikes with reptiles were reported: phase of flight not reported (75), taxi (5), takeoff run (11), approach (4; pilot had a missed approach because reptile was on the runway), and landing roll (5).

Table 9. Number of reported bird strikes to civil aircraft by height (feet) above ground level (AGL), USA, 1990–2008[1].

Height of strike (feet AGL)	All reported strikes			Strikes with damage		
	19-year total	% of total known	% cumulative total	19-year total	% of total known	% cumulative total
0	23,118	41	41	1,900	26	26
1-100	10,277	18	59	1,194	17	43
101-200	2,700	5	64	338	5	48
201-300	1,746	3	67	223	3	51
301-400	1,074	2	69	166	2	53
401-500	1,936	3	72	274	4	57
501-600	550	1	73	105	1	58
601-700	438	1	74	76	1	59
701-800	875	2	76	173	2	61
801-900	281	1	77	72	1	62
901-1,000	1,674	3	80	336	5	67
1,001-2,000	4,083	7	87	926	13	80
2,001-3,000	2,636	5	92	558	8	88
3,001-4,000	1,376	2	94	227	3	91
4,001-5,000	981	2	96	173	2	93
5,001-10,000	1,845	3	99	347	5	98
10,001-15,000	314	1	100	86	1	99
15,001-20,000	35	<1	100	21	<1	99
20,001-30,000	15	<1	100	9	<1	99
32,500	1	<1	100	1	<1	99
Total known	**55,955**	**100**		**7,205**	**100**	
Unknown height	**31,461**			**2,428**		
Total	**87,416**			**9,633**		

[1] A more detailed analysis of bird strikes by height AGL is provided by Dolbeer (2006*b*).

Table 10. Civil aircraft components reported as being struck and damaged by wildlife, USA, 1990–2008.

Aircraft component	Birds (19-year total)				Terrestrial mammals (19-year total)			
	Number struck	% of total	Number damaged	% of total	Number struck	% of total	Number damaged	% of total
Windshield	13,557	17	673	6	7	<1	13	1
Engine(s)[1]	11,616	15	3,596	32	131	8	140	10
Nose	11,361	14	674	6	78	4	78	6
Wing/rotor	10,510	13	2,594	23	199	11	209	15
Fuselage	9,947	12	435	4	106	6	117	8
Radome	9,925	12	1,114	10	13	1	14	1
Other	5,678	7	856	8	207	12	183	13
Landing gear	3,592	4	356	3	704	40	317	23
Propeller	2,049	3	206	2	224	13	213	15
Tail	1,078	1	453	4	48	3	63	5
Light	590	1	456	4	26	1	33	2
Total[2]	**79,903**	**100**	**11,413**	**100**	**1,743**	**100**	**1,380**	**100**

[1] For birds, 11,616 engines were reported as struck in 11,060 strike events involving engines (10,525 events with one engine struck, 518 with two engines struck, 12 with three engines struck, and 5 with four engines struck). A total of 3,596 engines was damaged in 3,484 bird-strike events with engine damage (3,375 events with one engine damaged, 107 with two engines damaged, 1 with three engines damaged, and 1 with 4 engines damaged). For terrestrial mammals, 131 engines were reported as struck in 122 strike events (113 events with one engine struck and 9 with two engines struck). A total of 140 engines was damaged in 124 terrestrial mammal strike events with engine damage (108 events with one engine damaged and 16 with two engines damaged). Some engines were damaged without being struck when the landing gear collapsed.

[2] In addition, bat strikes had 95 and 7 components reported as struck and damaged, respectively: radome/nose (27, 0), windshield (20, 0), engine (11, 3), propeller (1, 0), wing/rotor (12, 3), fuselage (8, 0), tail (2, 0), other (9, 0), landing gear (4, 0), light (1, 1). For reptile strikes, there were 20 and 5 components reported struck and damaged, respectively: windshield (1, 1), wing/rotor (1, 1), fuselage (1, 1), landing gear (15, 0); tail (1, 1), other (1, 1).

Table 11. Number of civil aircraft with reported damage resulting from wildlife strikes, USA, 1990–2008.

| Damage category[2] | Reported strikes | | | | | |
| | Birds | | Terrestrial mammals | | Total[1] | |
	19-year total	% of total known	19-year total	% of total known	19-year total	% of total known
None	**59,047**	**86**	**508**	**41**	**59,655**	**85**
Damage	**9,606**	**14**	**738**	**59**	**10,352**	**15**
Minor	5,112	7	324	26	5,439	8
Uncertain	2,015	3	58	5	2,074	3
Substantial	2,455	4	331	27	2,790	4
Destroyed	24	<1	25	2	49	<1
Total known	**68,653**	**100**	**1,246**	**100**	**70,007**	**100**
Unknown	**18,763**		**666**		**19,720**	
Total	**87,416**		**1,912**		**89,727**	

[1] Included in totals are 299 and 100 strikes involving bats and reptiles, respectively. For bats, 85 reports indicated no damage, 207 failed to report if damage occurred, 3 reported minor damage, 1 reported uncertain level of damage, and 3 reported substantial damage. For reptiles, 15 reports indicated no damage, 84 failed to report if damage occurred, and 1 reported substantial damage.

[2] The damage codes and descriptions follow the *International Civil Aviation Organization Bird Strike Information System (1989):* Minor = the aircraft can be rendered airworthy by simple repairs or replacements and an extensive inspection is not necessary; Uncertain = the aircraft was damaged, but details as to the extent of the damage are lacking; Substantial = the aircraft incurs damage or structural failure that adversely affects the structure strength, performance, or flight characteristics of the aircraft and that would normally require major repair or replacement of the affected component (specifically excluded are bent fairings or cowlings; small dents or puncture holes in the skin; damage to wing tips, antenna, tires, or brakes; and engine blade damage not requiring blade replacement); Destroyed = the damage sustained makes it inadvisable to restore the aircraft to an airworthy condition.

Table 12. Number of civil aircraft with reported damage resulting from bird and terrestrial mammal strikes by year, USA, 1990–2008[1,2].

	Strikes with damage (birds)					Strikes with damage (terrestrial mammals)			
Year	Minor or un-certain level	Sub-stantial	De-stroyed	Total		Minor or un-certain level	Sub-stantial	De-stroyed	Total
1990	224	103		327		3	8	1	12
1991	238	126		364		5	12		17
1992	204	106	3	313		17	22	1	40
1993	262	94		356		20	9	2	31
1994	268	135	4	407		29	14	1	44
1995	283	165		448		23	14		37
1996	278	170		448		28	26	2	56
1997	353	167		520		32	25	1	58
1998	400	131	2	533		34	16	3	53
1999	498	156		654		20	22		42
2000	551	153	1	705		33	23		56
2001	479	120		599		23	21	1	45
2002	511	120	1	632		13	22	1	36
2003	462	125	2	589		17	20	3	40
2004	439	133		572		20	18	3	41
2005	408	147	2	557		24	22	2	48
2006	441	119		560		17	13	2	32
2007	418	106	5	529		17	14		31
2008	410	79	4	493		7	10	2	19
Total	**7,127**	**2,455**	**24**	**9,606**		**382**	**331**	**25**	**738**

[1] In addition, 7 strike reports involving bats indicated damage (3 substantial and 4 minor or undetermined level). For reptiles, 1 strike report indicated substantial damage.

[2] See Table 11 for definitions of damage levels.

Table 13. Reported effect-on-flight (EOF) of wildlife strikes to civil aircraft, USA, 1990–2008.

| | Reported strikes | | | | | |
| | Birds | | Terrestrial mammals | | Total[1] | |
Effect-on-flight[2]	19-year total	% of total known	19-year total	% of total known	19-year total	% of total known
None	**45,517**	**88**	**478**	**48**	**46,083**	**87**
Negative effect	**6,390**	**12**	**525**	**52**	**6,924**	**13**
Precautionary landing	3,283	6	79	8	3,365	6
Aborted takeoff	1,514	3	170	17	1,684	3
Engine shutdown	321	1	26	3	347	1
Other	1,272	2	250	25	1,528	3
Total known	**51,907**	**100**	**1,003**	**100**	**53,007**	**100**
Unknown	**35,509**		**909**		**36,720**	
Total	**87,416**		**1,912**		**89,727**	

[1] Included in totals are 299 and 100 strikes involving bats and reptiles, respectively. For bats, 69 reports indicated no effect-on-flight, 228 failed to report if an effect-on-flight occurred, and 2 reported a precautionary landing. For reptiles, 19 reports indicated no effect-on-flight, 74 failed to report if an effect-on-flight occurred, 1 reported a precautionary landing, and 6 reported "other".

[2] Effect-on-flight: None = flight continued as scheduled, although delays and other cost caused by inspections or repairs may have been incurred after landing; Aborted takeoff = pilot aborted the takeoff; Precautionary landing = pilot landed at other-than-destination airport after strike; Engine shut down = pilot shut down the engine or the engine stopped running because of strike; Other = miscellaneous effects, such as reduced speed because of shattered windshield, emergency landing at destination airport, or crash landing; Unknown = report did not give sufficient information to determine an effect-on-flight (Dolbeer et al. 2000).

Table 14. Total reported strikes, strikes causing damage, strikes having a negative effect-on-flight (EOF), strikes involving >1 animal, aircraft downtime, and costs by identified wildlife species for civil aircraft, USA, 1990–2008 (page 1 of 16).

Wildlife group or species	19-year totals					
	Number of reported strikes				Reported economic losses[1]	
	Total	With damage	With neg. EOF	With multiple animals[2]	Aircraft down time (hrs)	Reported costs ($)
Birds						
Loons	**19**	**12**	**7**		**2,867**	**1,766,200**
Loons	3	3	2		557	251,200
Common loon	15	8	4		2,262	1,513,000
Red-throated loon	1	1	1		48	2,000
Grebes	**44**	**8**	**5**	**7**	**168**	**2,109,470**
Grebes	8	1		1		
Eared grebe	6	1		1	10	100,000
Western grebe	13	4	3	5	86	1,900,000
Pied-billed grebe	9		1			
Horned grebe	5	2	1		72	109,470
Red-necked grebe	2					
Clark's grebe	1					
Albatrosses/shearwaters	**49**	**7**	**6**		**149**	**62,500**
Laysan albatross	31	6	5		149	62,500
Black-footed albatross	4	1				
Bonin petrel	1					
Wedge-tailed shearwater	8		1			
Townsend's shearwater	4					
Fork-tailed storm-petrel	1					
Tropicbirds	**11**	**8**	**7**		**172**	**75,300**
Tropicbirds	5	5	4		124	40,200
White-tailed tropicbird	3	2	2		48	29,500
Red-tailed tropicbird	3	1	1			5,600
Pelicans	**53**	**26**	**21**	**8**	**422**	**2,351,123**
Pelicans	4	2			80	
Australian pelican	1	1	1			
Brown pelican	42	19	16	5	318	251,123
American white pelican	6	4	4	3	24	2,100,000
Red- footed booby	**1**					
Cormorants	**67**	**24**	**15**	**11**	**241**	**2,204,370**
Cormorants	5					
Great cormorant	2	1		2		
D.-crested cormorant	59	23	15	9	241	2,204,370
Pelagic cormorant	1					
Anhinga	**15**	**5**	**6**	**3**	**117**	**7,800**

Table 14. Continued (page 2 of 16).

Wildlife group or species	19-year totals					
	Number of reported strikes				Reported economic losses[1]	
	Total	With dam-age	With neg. EOF	With multiple animals[2]	Aircraft down time (hrs)	Reported costs ($)
Frigatebirds	**11**	**4**	**2**		**21**	**18,400**
Frigatebirds	2	1	1		18	13,500
Great frigatebird	7	2	1		3	4,900
Magnificent frigatebird	2	1				
Herons/bitterns	**360**	**67**	**48**	**12**	**3,426**	**4,861,610**
Herons	47	13	9	4	99	3,200
Great blue heron	213	47	36	4	2,647	4,766,024
Blk-crowned night-heron	33	3	1	2	16	31,200
Little blue heron	4					
Green heron	7					
Yel.-crowned night heron	6	1			18	17,000
American bittern	5	3	2		646	44,186
Yellow bittern	45			2		
Egrets	**490**	**56**	**68**	**125**	**3,717**	**5,318,690**
Egrets	268	30	39	76	3,455	3,465,140
Cattle egret	163	17	23	42	141	12,750
Great egret	38	7	6	6	97	1,840,800
Snowy egret	21	2		1	24	
Storks/ibises	**33**	**7**	**5**	**6**	**1**	
White stork	1	1				
Wood stork	9	2	1	1		
Ibises	11	1	2	1		
Glossy ibis	1			1		
White ibis	5	1	1	1		
White-faced ibis	5	2		2		
Roseate spoonbill	1		1		1	
Waterfowl	**3,175**	**1,418**	**694**	**1,159**	**110,135**	**101,332,546**
Ducks, geese, swans	133	63	30	53	715	758,775
Ducks	663	228	105	217	5,221	4,024,921
American wigeon	24	13	5	7	327	888,089
Northern pintail	47	31	17	25	1396	1,309,044
Green-winged teal	22	9	6	7	732	688,142
Blue-winged teal	15	8	3	8	145	608,440
European wigeon	1			1		
Mallard	473	120	60	107	8,479	5,129,911
Common eider	3	2	1	1		
Ring-necked duck	8	4	2	3	240	46,468
Greater scaup	4	1	1	1		

Table 14. Continued (page 3 of 16).

Wildlife group or species	19-year totals					
	Number of reported strikes				Reported economic losses[1]	
	Total	With dam-age	With neg. EOF	With multiple animals[2]	Aircraft down time (hrs)	Reported costs ($)
Wood duck	22	9	4	6	294	85,704
Muscovy duck	1	1			120	443,332
Common goldeneye	3	2	1			2,000
Red-breasted merganser	4	1		1	2	
Hooded merganser	3	1		1		
Common merganser	1	1	1		72	2,500
Northern shoveler	22	11	3	11	648	1,079,570
Gadwall	19	5	2	4	414	1,513,678
Canvasback	11	4	1	4	335	2,154,077
American black duck	27	3	1	8	36	1,500
Mottled duck	11	4	3	2	24	
Lesser scaup	16	10	6	7	999	111,000
Ruddy duck	12	4	1		24	8,446
Redhead	3	1		1		
Bufflehead	3					
Long-tailed duck	2	2	1			
Philippine duck	1	1	1	1	96	9,456,000
Blk.-bellied whistling duck	1					
Cinnamon teal	2					
White-winged scoter	1	1	1	1	1,400	430,000
Hawaiian duck	2					
Geese	310	189	82	112	24,328	2,000,117
Snow goose	78	62	29	41	4,213	17,041,554
Canada goose	1,181	603	317	509	59,087	50,902,670
Brant	18	8	3	7	88	51,271
Gr. white-fronted goose	13	9	3	8	292	1,500,547
Emperor goose	1					
Swans	2	1				
Mute swan	5			1		
Tundra swan	5	4	2	3	336	144,790
Trumpeter swan	2	2	2	1	72	950,000
Raptors	5,070	852	574	184	83,540	40,224,236
Hawks, eagles, vultures	29	16	7	1	2,559	17,550
Vultures	254	146	70	26	21,461	9,306,693
Black vulture	45	26	19	5	5,161	1,407,128
Turkey vulture	317	168	113	16	23,391	4,482,590
Osprey	148	36	22	3	2,268	292,923
White-tailed kite	12	3	1		40	5,000,000

Table 14. Continued (page 4 of 16).

Wildlife group or species	19-year totals					
	Number of reported strikes				Reported economic losses[1]	
	Total	With dam-age	With neg. EOF	With multiple animals[2]	Aircraft down time (hrs)	Reported costs ($)
Black kite	2	1	1			
Swallow-tailed kite	1					
Eagles	6	3	2	1		
Bald eagle	111	48	29	9	6,209	384,140
Wh.-breasted sea eagle	1	1	1			
Golden eagle	8	2	4		3,696	801,000
Hawks	975	195	138	25	9,241	3,865,084
Red-tailed hawk	965	160	116	16	8,434	5,721,618
Rough-legged hawk	34	1	1			167
Red-shouldered hawk	15	1	2		41	900
Swainson's hawk	46	4	3	1	8	
Sharp-shinned hawk	11					
Cooper's hawk	31	2	1			
Ferruginous hawk	8	1	1		24	3,200,000
Broad-winged hawk	8	1				
Harris' hawk	2					
Common buzzard	1				24	
Northern harrier	65	2	1	1		200,000
Lappet-faced vulture	1	1	1		240	4,000,000
Falcons	37	3	3	1	81	30,000
Peregrine falcon	135	10	3	6	78	235,500
Gyrfalcon	1					
Merlin	34		2		3	130
Crested caracara	4	2	1		2	
Prairie falcon	8					
American kestrel	1,751	18	31	73	579	1,278,813
Eurasian kestrel	4	1	1			
Gallinaceous birds	**150**	**40**	**33**	**28**	**1,820**	**612,287**
Grouse	7	2		3	2	
Greater sage grouse	5	3	4	1	337	256,077
Sharp-tailed grouse	1	1	1		24	500
Ptarmigans	6	4	1	2	57	57,500
Black francolin	2					
Quails	10		2	2		
Northern bobwhite	6	2	3	1	73	800
Scaled quail	3					
Ring-necked pheasant	56	12	9	5	855	84,000
Partridges	1					

Table 14. Continued (page 5 of 16).

Wildlife group or species	19-year totals					
	Number of reported strikes				Reported economic losses[1]	
	Total	With damage	With neg. EOF	With multiple animals[2]	Aircraft down time (hrs)	Reported costs ($)
Red-legged partridge	1					
Gray partridge	5	2	1	3	24	120
Chukar	2		1	1		
Grey francolin	1					
Guineafowl	1	1		1		
Wild turkey	43	13	11	9	448	213,290
Cranes	**92**	**35**	**28**	**30**	**2,369**	**434,560**
Cranes	12	3	5	2	31	250,000
Sandhill crane	79	31	23	28	2,290	134,260
Whooping crane	1	1			48	50,300
Rails/gallinules	**86**	**18**	**8**	**6**	**1,013**	**957,926**
Rails	3	1	1	1		
Sora	3					
Common moorhen	2	1	1		24	990
American coot	69	15	5	5	917	931,486
Purple gallinule	3	1	1		72	25,450
Virginia rail	2					
Clapper rail	4					
Shorebirds	**2,604**	**68**	**99**	**446**	**1,317**	**3,024,581**
Shorebirds	17			8		
American oystercatcher	18			2		
Plovers	39	3	4	8	24	
European golden-plover	3					
American golden-plover	49	1	3	16	16	2,000
Black-bellied plover	41	2	2	6	12	38,622
Snowy plover	1			1		
Killdeer	1,421	31	40	150	288	2,386,113
Pacific golden-plover	472	3	9	77	35	2,200
Semipalmated plover	27			11		
Wilson's plover	1					
Northern lapwing	1	1	1	1	25	
Southern lapwing	1	1	1			8,000
Sandpipers	163	9	20	64	169	106,560
Upland sandpiper	97	4	6	12	12	1,000
Spotted sandpiper	6			2		
Willett	5			2		
Common snipe	28	2	1	3		12,615
American woodcock	23	1	2	3		

Table 14. Continued (page 6 of 16).

Wildlife group or species	19-year totals					
	Number of reported strikes				Reported economic losses[1]	
	Total	With damage	With neg. EOF	With multiple animals[2]	Aircraft down time (hrs)	Reported costs ($)
Dunlin	14	3	2	5	504	205,300
Baird's sandpiper	8			1		
Western sandpiper	37	1	1	23	60	94,311
Pectoral sandpiper	4	1		2		300
Sanderling	15		1	8		
Buff-breasted sandpiper	13			4		
Ruddy turnstone	4					
Least sandpiper	32	1	3	14	3	
Semipalmated sandpiper	25			10		
Lesser yellowlegs	3			1		
Short-billed dowitcher	5	1		1		
Hudsonian godwit	1	1	1	1	96	23,495
Solitary sandpiper	2			1		
Greater yellowlegs	1					
Long-billed dowitcher	4			2	1	
Red knot	2					
White-rumped sandpiper	1					
Black turnstone	1					
Marbled godwit	1	1	1	1	48	144,065
Curlews	1			1		
Whimbrel	6	1	1	1	24	
Long-billed curlew	3					
Red-necked phalarope	2					
American avocet	3			2		
Black-necked stilt	3			2		
Gulls/jaegers	**7,470**	**1,169**	**935**	**1,791**	**48,320**	**35,839,010**
Parasitic jaeger	1					
Gulls	5,380	945	737	1,437	35,062	19,041,746
Herring gull	715	80	75	85	1,813	1,668,351
Mew gull	41	6	4	6	17	86,717
Ring-billed gull	805	81	71	168	4,955	2,898,660
Glaucous-winged gull	56	12	7	10	290	346,545
Great black-backed gull	67	7	5	4	27	250,000
Franklin's gull	37	3	3	16	18	139,000
Laughing gull	233	16	18	41	731	534,136
Bonaparte's gull	20	2	2	6		65,000
Lesser black-backed gull	1					
Western gull	61	7	4	7	92	540,857

Table 14. Continued (page 7 of 16).

Wildlife group or species	19-year totals					
	Number of reported strikes				Reported economic losses[1]	
	Total	With damage	With neg. EOF	With multiple animals[2]	Aircraft down time (hrs)	Reported costs ($)
California gull	44	7	6	6	4,859	361,948
Heermann's gull	1			1		
Thayer's gull	3					
Yellow-legged gull	3	3	3	3	456	9,906,050
Glaucous gull	2			1		
Terns/kittiwakes	**107**	**4**	**3**	**24**	**4**	
Terns	38	2		12		
Caspian tern	17			1		
Common tern	11			1		
Gull-billed tern	1					
Fairy tern	1					
White tern	1		1	1		
Arctic tern	3	1		2		
Roseate tern	1					
Forster's tern	5		1	1	4	
Least tern	7			2		
Black noddy	3			2		
Brown noddy	6		1	1		
Royal tern	2					
Sooty tern	1					
Black-legged kittiwake	2					
Red-legged kittiwake	1					
Black skimmer	7	1		1		
Pigeons/doves	**5,590**	**341**	**400**	**1,447**	**22,388**	**11,250,886**
Pigeons, doves	12	1	1	8	24	400
Pigeons	26	4	4	12	32	46,050
Doves	837	42	74	237	1,096	293,610
Rock pigeon	1,588	183	166	562	13,841	5,146,449
Racing pigeon (banded)	18	4	2	8	144	16,000
Mourning dove	2,893	102	148	604	7,117	5,473,972
Spotted dove	73	3	3	4	132	274,405
Zebra dove	101	2	2	12	2	
Inca dove	14					
Philippine turtle dove	4					
White-winged dove	18					
Common ground-dove	6					
Parrots	**12**			**1**		
Parrots	6			1		

Table 14. Continued (page 8 of 16).

Wildlife group or species	19-year totals					
	Number of reported strikes				Reported economic losses[1]	
	Total	With dam-age	With neg. EOF	With multiple animals[2]	Aircraft down time (hrs)	Reported costs ($)
Budgerigar	5					
Black-hooded parakeet	1					
Cuckoos	**11**	**1**		**3**		
Cuckoos	1			1		
Yellow-billed cuckoo	9	1		2		
Common cuckoo	1					
Owls	**1,168**	**81**	**53**	**9**	**1,465**	**4,026,013**
Owls	252	29	15	4	960	296,875
Barn owl	504	23	19	4	248	1,900,310
Snowy owl	54	5	5		46	27,500
Short-eared owl	186	6	5		17	845
Long-eared owl	8	2	1			
Northern saw-whet owl	4					
Burrowing owl	66	1			1	
Barred owl	7	1	1			
Northern pygmy-owl	1					
Eastern screech owl	2	1			24	7,558
Western screech owl	2					
Great horned owl	82	13	7	1	169	1,792,925
Nightjars	**163**	**2**		**9**		
Nightjars	4	1				
Whip-poor-will	2					
Common poorwill	6					
Lesser nighthawk	6					
Chuck-will's-widow	1					
Common nighthawk	144	1		9		
Swifts	**107**	**3**	**2**	**7**		
Swifts	9	1		2		
Chimney swift	79	1	2	5		
Vaux's swift	11					
White-throated swift	8	1				
Hummingbirds	**4**					
Hummingbirds	2					
R.-throated hummingbird	1					
Anna's hummingbird	1					
Belted kingfisher	**7**					
Woodpeckers	**48**	**2**	**4**	**1**	**1**	**15,000**
Woodpeckers	9		1			

Table 14. Continued (page 9 of 16).

Wildlife group or species	19-year totals					
	Number of reported strikes				Reported economic losses[1]	
	Total	With damage	With neg. EOF	With multiple animals[2]	Aircraft down time (hrs)	Reported costs ($)
Northern flicker	29	2				
Yellow-bellied sapsucker	5		1	1		
Hairy woodpecker	3					
Red-naped sapsucker	1		1			15,000
Downy woodpecker	1		1		1	
Flycatchers	**121**	**1**	**4**	**9**	**1**	**9,800**
Tyrant flycatchers	9			1	1	
Eastern wood-pewee	3					
Great crested flycatcher	1					
Eastern kingbird	8	1	1			9,800
Scissor-tailed flycatcher	42		2	4		
Acadian flycatcher	1					
Say's phoebe	2					
Western kingbird	50		1	3		
Ash-throated flycatcher	1					
Western wood-pewee	1					
Sulphur-bellied flycatcher	1					
Eastern phoebe	1					
Yellow-bellied flycatcher	1			1		
Larks	**902**	**10**	**14**	**225**	**62**	**505,625**
Larks	5			1		
Eurasian skylark	14			1		
Horned lark	883	10	14	223	62	505,625
Swallows	**1,964**	**15**	**39**	**472**	**137**	**37,522**
Swallows	504	4	24	162	26	
Purple martin	77	2	1	20	3	
Bank swallow	90	2	3	42	5	
Barn swallow	828	4	6	143	89	23,807
Cliff swallow	275	3	2	46	9	13,650
Tree swallow	169		3	58	5	65
Violet-green swallow	9			1		
N. rough-winged swallow	12					
Starlings/mynas	**2,115**	**89**	**122**	**827**	**1,494**	**4,326,605**
European starling	2,070	88	121	815	1,490	4,326,605
Mynas	4			2		
Common myna	41	1	1	10	4	
Crows/jays/magpies	**509**	**53**	**47**	**75**	**6,609**	**1,478,158**
Crows	218	22	21	34	905	144,000

39

Table 14. Continued (page 10 of 16).

Wildlife group or species	19-year totals					
	Number of reported strikes				Reported economic losses[1]	
	Total	With damage	With neg. EOF	With multiple animals[2]	Aircraft down time (hrs)	Reported costs ($)
American crow	236	21	19	34	5,562	1,265,113
Carrion crow	1					
Hooded crow	1	1	1			
Northwestern crow	2			1		
Blue jay	9					
Common raven	26	7	4	2	141	68,490
Yellow-billed magpie	8			2		
Black-billed magpie	8	2	2	2	1	555
Chickadees	**21**	**1**		**7**		
Chickadees	5	1		2		
Black-capped chickadee	13			2		
Mountain chickadee	2			2		
Gray-headed chickadee	1			1		
Wrens	**49**	**1**	**2**	**8**		
Wrens	39	1	1	8		
Marsh wren	3		1			
House wren	4					
Carolina wren	1					
Rock wren	1					
Cactus wren	1					
Mimics	**76**	**1**	**2**	**3**		**120**
Brown thrasher	8					120
Curve-billed thrasher	1					
Northern mockingbird	45	1	2			
Gray catbird	22			3		
Thrushes	**348**	**29**	**20**	**31**	**1,600**	**2,352,140**
Thrushes	16	3	1	2	7	25,500
Western bluebird	2				3	
Swainson's thrush	16	2	1	2	1	2,000,025
American robin	283	20	15	25	1,565	313,630
Hermit thrush	10	1			22	3,800
Eastern bluebird	3					
Gray-cheeked thrush	1					
Varied thrush	13	3	2	1	2	8,905
Wood thrush	4		1	1		280
Kinglets	**7**					
Golden-crowned kinglet	2					
Ruby-crowned kinglet	5					

Table 14. Continued (page 11 of 16).

Wildlife group or species	19-year totals					
	Number of reported strikes				Reported economic losses[1]	
	Total	With damage	With neg. EOF	With multiple animals[2]	Aircraft down time (hrs)	Reported costs ($)
Wrentits/gnatcatchers	**2**					
Wrentit	1					
Blue-gray gnatcatcher	1					
Vireos	**11**	**1**		**2**		
Vireos	2					
Yellow-throated vireo	1					
Warbling vireo	3			1		
Red-eyed vireo	4	1		1		
Cassin's vireo	1					
Warblers	**98**	**3**	**4**	**6**	**164**	**343**
Wood warblers	23			1		
Canada warbler	3					
Yellow-breasted chat	4					
Pine warbler	2					
Black and white warbler	3					
Northern parula warbler	2					
Ovenbird	7	1	2		1	100
Wilson's warbler	6					
Common yellowthroat	6					
Yellow-rumped warbler	12			2		43
Blackpoll warbler	3			2	1	200
American redstart	1				3	
Orange-crowned warbler	1					
Yellow warbler	3	1			15	
Northern waterthrush	2					
Nashville warbler	7	1	2	1	144	
Townsend's warbler	1					
Palm warbler	4					
Magnolia warbler	4					
Blk-throated blue warbler	2					
Prothonotary warbler	1					
MacGillivray's warbler	1					
Meadowlarks	**882**	**10**	**19**	**102**	**228**	**266,452**
Meadowlarks	208	2	6	16	10	
Eastern meadowlark	400	3	5	38	4	
Western meadowlark	274	5	8	48	214	266,452
Blackbirds/orioles	**1,426**	**89**	**99**	**399**	**1,464**	**1,046,730**
Blackbirds	1,066	73	78	323	587	862,825

Table 14. Continued (page 12 of 16).

Wildlife group or species	19-year totals					
	Number of reported strikes				Reported economic losses[1]	
	Total	With damage	With neg. EOF	With multiple animals[2]	Aircraft down time (hrs)	Reported costs ($)
Red-winged blackbird	89	2	6	13	7	750
Yellow-headed blackbird	6	1	1	1		
Brewer's blackbird	25			2		
Brown-headed cowbird	75	1	2	25	6	5,155
Bobolink	6			1		
Rusty blackbird	1					
Orioles	5					
Baltimore oriole	4			1		
Orchard oriole	1					
Bullock's oriole	1					
Grackles	71	5	3	18	720	133,000
Common grackle	58	5	6	14	123	45,000
Boat-tailed grackle	5	1	1		20	
Great-tailed grackle	10			2		
Scarlet tanager	2	1				
Western tanager	1		1		1	
Finches/buntings	**288**	**5**	**22**	**112**	**76**	**9,000**
Finches	53		5	15	4	
Lapland longspur	6			3		
Chest.-collared longspur	1					
Dark-eyed junco	15	2	2	2	49	9,000
Rose-breasted grosbeak	2					
Pine siskin	3			2	1	
Purple finch	1					
Evening grosbeak	1					
American goldfinch	24		1	1		
House finch	34			4		
Smith's longspur	1					
Dickcissel	1					
White-winged crossbill	1					
Red avadavat	2			1		
Lesser goldfinch	1					
Red-crested cardinal	2			1		
Northern cardinal	3					
Snow bunting	114	2	14	79	20	
Indigo bunting	1					
Lazuli bunting	1					
Lark bunting	21	1		4	2	

Table 14. Continued (page 13 of 16).

| Wildlife group or species | 19-year totals | | | | | |
| | Number of reported strikes | | | | Reported economic losses[1] | |
	Total	With damage	With neg. EOF	With multiple animals[2]	Aircraft down time (hrs)	Reported costs ($)
Sparrows	**2,358**	**44**	**91**	**580**	**595**	**53,340**
Sparrows	2,142	41	89	559	589	47,840
Harris' sparrow	1					
Swamp sparrow	4					
Savannah sparrow	87	1		7	3	1,000
Fox sparrow	11	1				4,100
White-throated sparrow	17	1	1	2		
Golden-crowned sparrow	3			1		
Field sparrow	6					
Lark sparrow	8					
White-crowned sparrow	7					
Grasshopper sparrow	13		1	1		
Java sparrow	2			1		
Vesper sparrow	4			1		
Chipping sparrow	9			1		
Lincoln's sparrow	4					
Song sparrow	31			7	3	400
Sage sparrow	3					
American tree sparrow	6					
Towhees	**4**					
Rufous-sided towhee	3					
Green-tailed towhee	1					
Mannikins	**95**		**1**	**47**	**8**	**3,600**
Mannikins	23			11		
Nutmeg mannikin	31			16	6	1,600
Chestnut mannikin	41		1	20	2	2,000
Misc. perching birds	**181**	**9**	**5**	**27**	**54**	**87,100**
Perching birds	83	8	3	12	50	87,100
House sparrow	58	1		9		
Cedar waxwing	17		1	3	4	
American pipit	12			1		
Loggerhead shrike	5		1			
Common waxbill	3					
Warbling silverbill	1			1		
Japanese white-eye	1					
Red-vented bulbul	1			1		

Table 14. Continued (page 14 of 16).

Wildlife group or species	19-year totals					
	Number of reported strikes				Reported economic losses[1]	
	Total	With damage	With neg. EOF	With multiple animals[2]	Aircraft down time (hrs)	Reported costs ($)
Total known birds	38,474	4,619	3,514	8,249	296,165	226,669,043
Total unknown birds	48,942	4,987	2,876	5,319	97,356	81,643,958
Unknown bird - ? size	23,014	2,565	1,252	1,447	27,300	29,635,466
Unknown bird-large	1,853	799	377	212	28,539	29,195,971
Unknown bird-medium	6,432	1017	551	893	32,455	10,951,800
Unknown bird-small	17,643	606	696	2,767	9,062	11,860,721
Total birds[3]	87,416	9,606	6,390	13,568	393,521	308,313,001
Flying mammals (bats)						
Old world fruit bats	5	1	2	1	72	3,069,400
Vesper bats	1					
Red bat	17	1		1	1	
Hoary bat	2					
East. small-footed myotis	1					
Little brown bat	15					
Big brown bat	3					
Silver-haired bat	1					
Free-tailed bats	7			1		
Brazilian free-tailed bat	26					
Pocketed free-tailed bat	1					
Total known bats	79	2	2	3	73	3,069,400
Total unknown bats	220	5		21	27	106,440
Total bats[4]	299	7	2	24	100	3,175,840
Terrestrial mammals						
Marsupials (opossum)	66					
Xenarthyras (armadillo)	17	1	2		8	700
Lagomorphs	229	6	8	4	20	104,484
Black-tailed jackrabbit	81	2	1			24,384
White-tailed jackrabbit	19			1	1	
Rabbits	86	2	3	3	13	2,100
Eastern cottontail	43	2	4		6	78,000
Rodents	126	2	2	4	3	
Pocket gophers	2					
Squirrels	1					
Prairie dog	20		1	4		
Woodchuck	82	2	1		3	
Woodrats	2					

Table 14. Continued (page 15 of 16).

Wildlife group or species	19-year totals					
	Number of reported strikes				Reported economic losses[1]	
	Total	With damage	With neg. EOF	With multiple animals[2]	Aircraft down time (hrs)	Reported costs ($)
Muskrat	9					
N. American porcupine	10					
Carnivores	**641**	**44**	**94**	**9**	**13,949**	**3,112,976**
Canids	3		1			
Coyote	283	28	62	4	11,679	2,776,040
Domestic dog	29	8	16	1	96	301,000
Foxes	64	4	5	1	10	750
Red fox	54		5			
Common gray fox	4	1	1		2	186
Raccoon	58	2	3	2	2,160	35,000
White-nosed coati	1					
Ringtail	1					
Skunks	56		1		2	
Striped skunk	62			1		
River otter	2	1				
Badger	2					
Mink	1					
Domestic cat	18					
Small Indian mongoose	3					
Artiodactyls	**815**	**675**	**410**	**77**	**229,080**	**35,527,187**
Deer	16	13	10		696	197,000
White-tailed deer	729	601	357	67	194,967	28,739,056
Mule deer	37	32	20	3	10,512	751,827
Wapiti (elk)	9	9	6	2	11,560	5,496,204
Moose	4	3	4			
Caribou	2	2	1			
Cattle	8	8	6	2	6,215	187,000
Pronghorn	7	6	5	2	5,130	156,100
Swine (pigs)	1					
Collared peccary	2	1	1	1		
Perissodactyls	**4**	**4**	**3**		**1,008**	**23,849**
Horse	3	3	3		1,008	23,849
Burro	1	1				
Total known t. mammals	**1,898**	**732**	**519**	**94**	**244,068**	**38,769,196**
Total unknown t. mammal	**14**	**6**	**6**	**1**		
Total terrestrial mammals[5]	**1,912**	**738**	**525**	**95**	**244,068**	**38,769,196**

Table 14. Continued (page 16 of 16).

Wildlife group or species	19-year totals					
	Number of reported strikes				Reported economic losses[1]	
	Total	With damage	With neg. EOF	With multiple animals[2]	Aircraft down time (hrs)	Reported costs ($)
Reptiles						
Turtles	**79**		**2**	**1**		
Turtles	47		2	1		
Florida soft shell turtle	4					
Eastern box turtle	4					
Common snapping turtle	3					
Diamondback terrapin	19					
Painted turtle	2					
American alligator	**14**	**1**	**2**		**3**	
Green iguana	**7**		**3**			
Total reptiles	**100**	**1**	**7**	**1**	**3**	
Total known (all species)	40,551	5,354	4,042	8,347	540,309	268,507,639
Total (unknown species)	49,176	4,998	2,882	5,341	97,383	81,750,398
Grand total	89,727	10,352	6,924	13,688	637,692	350,258,037

[1] These reported economic losses by species and species groups should be considered as relative indices of losses and not as actual estimated losses. Only about 20 percent of strikes involving civil aircraft are reported and only about 44 percent of reported strikes identify the wildlife species or species group responsible. Furthermore, less than 25 percent of reported strikes indicating damage also provided an estimate of the cost of damage or the downtime (see Table 18). Finally, even when cost estimates were provided, many reports were filed before aircraft damage had been fully assessed. See Table 18 for a more detailed projection of actual economic losses.

[2] More than 1 animal was struck by the aircraft.

[3] Of the 87,416 reported bird strikes, 38,474 (44 percent) identified the bird at least to species group. Of the 38,474 reports with birds identified to species group, 24,351 (63 percent) identified the bird to exact species (381 species total of which 176 caused damage). Thus, the bird was identified to species in 28 percent of the reported strikes.

[4] Of the 299 reported bat strikes, 79 (26 percent) identified the bat at least to species group. Of the 79 reports with bats identified to species group, 66 (84 percent) identified the bat to exact species (8 species total of which 1 caused damage). Thus, the bat was identified to species in 22 percent of the reported strikes.

[5] Of the 1,912 reported terrestrial mammal strikes, 1,898 (99 percent) identified the mammal at least to species group. Of the 1,898 reports with mammals identified to species group, 1,667 (88 percent) identified the mammal to exact species (33 species total of which 19 caused damage). Thus, the mammal was identified to species in 87 percent of the reported strikes.

Table 15. Number of reported strikes, strikes with damage, and strikes having a negative effect-on-flight (EOF) for the four most commonly struck bird groups and three most commonly struck terrestrial mammal groups, civil aircraft, USA, 1990–2008.

Species group[1]	Reported strikes		Strikes with damage		Strikes with EOF	
	19-year total	% of total known	19-year total	% of total known	19-year total	% of total known
Birds						
Gulls	7,470	19	1,169	25	935	27
Pigeons/ doves	5,590	15	341	7	400	11
Raptors	5,070	13	852	18	574	16
Waterfowl	3,175	8	1,418	31	694	20
All other known	17,169	45	839	18	911	26
Total known birds	**38,474**	**100**	**4,619**	**100**	**3,514**	**100**
Unknown birds	**48,942**		**4,987**		**2,876**	
Total birds	**87,416**		**9,606**		**6,390**	
Terrestrial mammals						
Artiodactyls	815	43	675	92	410	79
Carnivores	641	34	44	6	94	18
Lagomorphs	229	12	6	1	8	2
All other known	213	11	7	1	7	1
Total known t. mammals	**1,898**	**100**	**732**	**100**	**519**	**100**
Unknown t. mammals	**14**		**6**		**6**	
Total t. mammals	**1,912**		**738**		**525**	

[1] See Table 14 for listing of species within each species group.

Table 16. Number of strikes to civil aircraft causing human fatality or injury and number of injuries and fatalities by wildlife species, USA, 1990–2008.

Species of wildlife	No. of strikes	No. of humans		Species of wildlife	No. of strikes	No. of humans
Strikes causing fatalities				**Strikes causing injuries (continued)**		
Unknown bird	5	7		American coot	2	2
Amer. white pelican	1	5		Rock pigeon	2	2
Canada goose	1	2		American kestrel	1	2
Brown pelican	1	1		Spotted dove	1	2
White-tailed deer	1	1		Domestic dog	1	2
Total (fatalities)	**9**	**16**		Mule deer	1	1
				Sharp-tailed grouse	1	1
Strikes causing injuries				Eastern cottontail	1	1
Unknown bird	35	40		Horse	1	1
White-tailed deer	17	24		Western grebe	1	1
Canada goose	15	18		Horned grebe	1	1
Ducks	13	15		Tropicbirds	1	1
Turkey vulture	11	13		Red-tailed tropicbird	1	1
Vultures	9	9		D.-crested cormorant	1	1
Gulls	8	9		Great frigatebird	1	1
Geese	7	7		Egrets	1	1
Red-tailed hawk	4	5		Lesser scaup	1	1
Black vulture	4	4		Long-tailed duck	1	1
Hawks	3	5		Snow goose	1	1
Herring gull	3	3		Sandhill crane	1	1
Ring-billed gull	2	8		Doves	1	1
Golden eagle	2	4		Mourning dove	1	1
Cattle	2	3		Owls	1	1
Anhinga	2	2		Sparrows	1	1
Mallard	2	2				
Osprey	2	2		**Total (injuries)**	**167**	**209**

Table 17. Number of civil aircraft lost (destroyed or damaged beyond repair) after striking wildlife by wildlife species and aircraft mass category, USA, 1990-2008[1].

Wildlife species or species group	Aircraft[2] mass category (Maximum takeoff mass)				Total aircraft lost
	≤2,250 kg	2,251-5,700 kg	5,701-27,000 kg	>27,000 kg	
White-tailed deer	13	5	1		19
Unknown bird	8	1	1		10
Canada goose	1	3			4
Cattle	1	1			2
Vulture[3]	3				3
Amer. white pelican		1			1
Bald eagle	1				1
Brown pelican	1				1
Coyote			1		1
Domestic dog	1				1
Eastern cottontail	1				1
Eurasian kestrel				1	1
Hawk	1				1
Mourning dove			1		1
Ring-billed gull		1			1
Wapiti (elk)			1		1
Total	**31**	**12**	**5**	**1**	**49**

[1] Thirty-three (67 percent) of the 49 wildlife strikes resulting in a destroyed aircraft occurred at General Aviation airports, 9 occurred away from an airport, 6 occurred at USA airports certificated for passenger service under 14 CFR Part 139, and 1 occurred at a foreign airport certificated for passenger service.

[2] Engine types on the 49 destroyed aircraft were piston (36), turbofan (5), turbojet (2), turboprop (5), and turboshaft (1). Aircraft operator was business (25), private (21), and commercial transport (3).

[3] Two turkey vultures and 1 unknown species of vulture (either turkey or black).

Table 18. Number of reported wildlife strikes indicating damage or a negative effect-on-flight (EOF) and reported losses in hours of downtime and U.S. dollars, for civil aircraft, USA, 1990–2008.

	Number of reports			Reported time (hours) aircraft out of service (No. of reports)	Cost in millions of dollars ($) (Number of reports)		
	Total reports	Reports indicating adverse effect	Reports indicating aircraft damage	Reports indicating negative EOF		Direct cost	Other cost	Total cost
19-yr total	89,727	15,179	10,352	6,924	637,692 (4,301)	308,603 (2,620)	41,655 (1,157)	350,258
19-yr avg.	4,722	799	545	364	33,563 (238)	16.242 (138)	2.219 (61)	18.435
Mean losses per incident reported					**148.3**	**0.118**	**0.036**	**0.154**
Estimated annual losses								
Minimum[1]					**118,448**	**94.100**	**28.762**	**122.862**
Maximum[2]					**592,245**	**470.498**	**143.812**	**614.311**

[1] Minimum values are based on the assumption that all 15,179 reported strikes indicating an adverse effect (negative EOF and/or damage) to aircraft (mean of 799/year) incurred similar amounts of damage and/or downtime and that these reports are all of the adverse-effect strikes that occurred.

[2] Maximum values are based on the assumption that the 15,179 reported strikes indicating an adverse effect represent only 20 percent of the total strikes that occurred (Cleary et al. 2005, Wright and Dolbeer 2005).

This page intentionally left blank

Figures

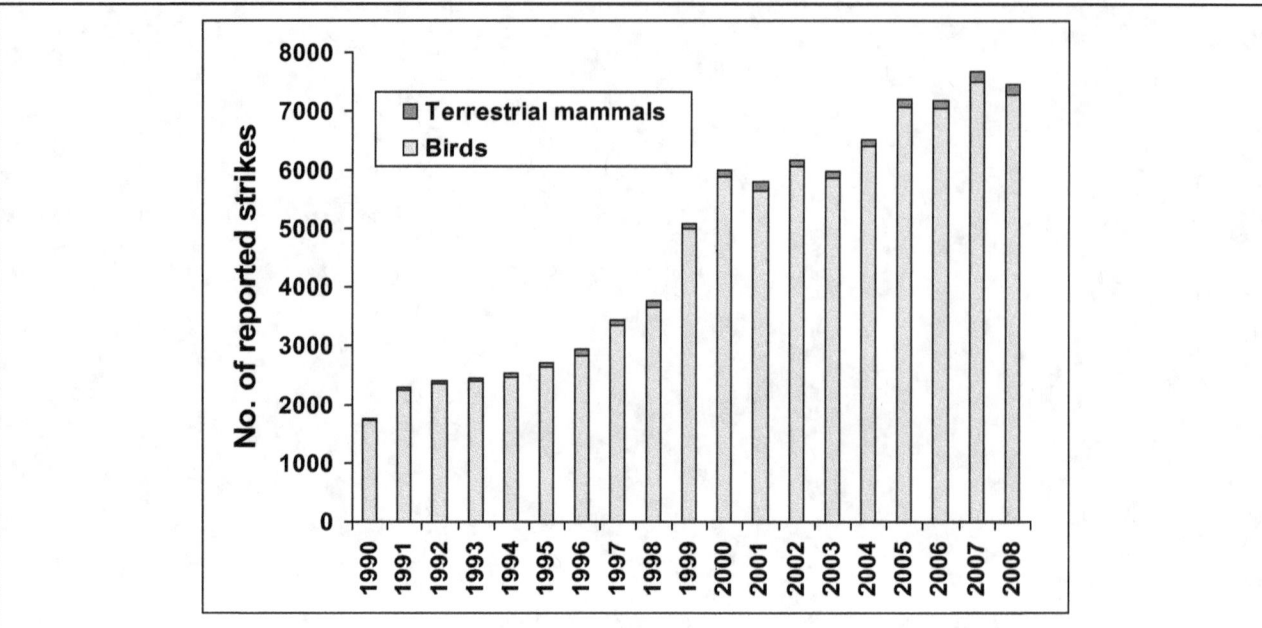

Figure 1. Number of reported bird (N = 87,416) and terrestrial mammal (N = 1,912) strikes to civil aircraft, USA, 1990–2008. Additionally, 299 and 100 strikes involving bats and reptiles, respectively, were reported for a total of 89,727 strikes by all species of wildlife (see Table 1).

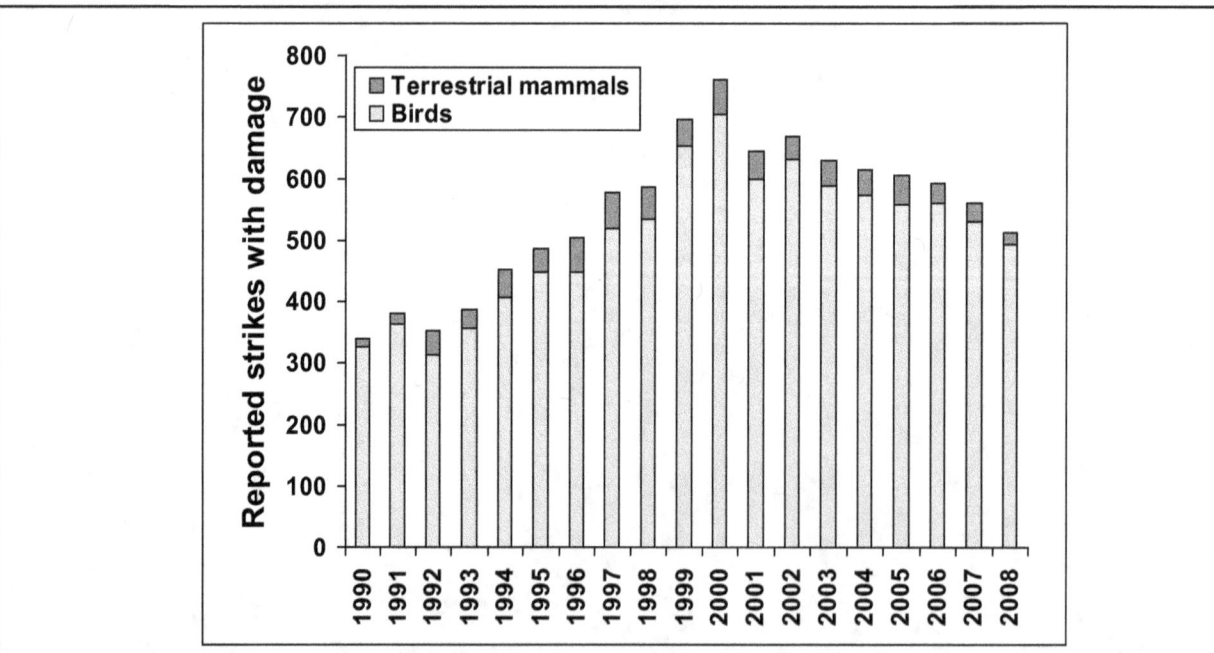

Figure 2. Number of reported bird (N = 9,606) and terrestrial mammal (N = 738) strikes causing damage to civil aircraft, USA, 1990–2008. Additionally, 7 and 1 damaging strikes involving bats and reptiles, respectively, were reported for a total of 10,352 damaging strikes by all species of wildlife (see Tables 11 and 12).

This page intentionally left blank

APPENDIX A.

SELECTED SIGNIFICANT WILDLIFE STRIKES TO U.S. CIVIL AIRCRAFT, 2008

A U.S.-based Air Cargo Boeing 747 overran the runway at Brussels International Airport, Belgium, after a rejected takeoff due to a Eurasian kestrel ingestion into the #3 engine, 25 May 2008. The plane broke into 3 pieces. None of the 5 people on board was seriously injured. This was 1 of 6 U.S. civil aircraft destroyed by wildlife strikes in 2008.

The U.S. Department of Agriculture, through an interagency agreement with the Federal Aviation Administration, compiles a database of all reported wildlife strikes to U.S. civil aircraft and to foreign carriers experiencing strikes in the USA. We compiled 89,727 strike reports from 1,456 USA airports and 215 foreign airports for 1990 through 2008 (7,516 strikes in 2008). The following examples from the database in 2008 are presented to show the serious impact that strikes by birds or other wildlife can have on aircraft. These examples, from throughout the USA, demonstrate the widespread and diverse nature of the problem. The examples are not intended to highlight or criticize individual airports because strikes have occurred on almost every airport in the USA. Some of the strike examples reported here occurred off airport property during approach or departure. For more information on wildlife strikes or to report a strike, visit *www.birdstrike.org* and *http://wildlife-mitigation.tc.faa.gov*.

Date:	26 January 2008
Aircraft:	BD-700
Airport:	Palm Beach Intl. (FL)
Phase of Flight:	Climb (2,500' AGL)
Effect on Flight:	Precautionary landing
Damage:	Engine
Wildlife Species:	Turkey vulture
Comments from Report:	Six fan blades, fan shroud and the engine inlet were damaged. The engine continued to run with no apparent problems. Time out of service was 14 days. Costs totaled $1,563,000.

Date:	29 January 2008
Aircraft:	B-747-200
Airport:	Louisville Intl. (KY)
Phase of Flight:	Climb
Effect on Flight:	Vibration and noise
Damage:	Engine
Wildlife Species:	Short-eared owl
Comments from Report:	Flight crew reported minor noise and vibration shortly after lift-off, which later subsided. Damage was found to 3 fan blades on the #2 engine. A piece of a liberated fan blade penetrated the cowl. Six fan blade pairs, the fan case outer-front acoustic panel and inlet cowl were replaced. ID by Smithsonian, Division of Birds.

Date:	4 March 2008
Aircraft:	Cessna Citation I
Airport:	Wiley Post (OK)
Phase of Flight:	Climb (3,100' AGL)
Effect on Flight:	Crashed
Damage:	Destroyed
Wildlife Species:	American white pelican
Comments from Report:	Witnesses saw the aircraft fly through a flock of birds, heard the engine compressor stall and watched the plane spiral, crash and burn. The NTSB investigated. ID by Smithsonian, Division of Birds. There were five fatalities.

Date:	10 March 2008
Aircraft:	Airbus 318
Airport:	Denver Intl. (CO)
Phase of Flight:	Approach (500' AGL)
Effect on Flight:	Emergency landing
Damage:	Landing gear, nose cowl
Wildlife Species:	Canada goose
Comments from Report:	Hit a flock of Canada geese on 1 mile final. Aircraft went around, declared an emergency due to smoke in cockpit and damage to aircraft. Loss of fluids was reported near taxiway and also brake and hydraulic problems. Aircraft had to be moved by tug to gate. Nose cowl was dented and both engines were struck. At least one engine ingested a bird. Time out of service was reported as a minimum of 16 hours. ID by Smithsonian, Division of Birds.

Date:	12 March 2008
Aircraft:	Bell-407
Airport:	Miami, FL
Phase of Flight:	En Route (600' AGL)
Effect on Flight:	Emergency landing
Damage:	Windshield
Wildlife Species:	Turkey vulture
Comments from Report:	Helicopter hit bird over Biscayne Bay about 6 miles east of MIA. It landed safely at MIA. Pilot was transported to the hospital by Fire and Rescue due to cuts and lacerations to his face caused by the broken windshield. Bird remains entered the cockpit. ID by Smithsonian, Division of Birds.

Date:	8 April 2008
Aircraft:	Challenger 600
Airport:	Colorado Springs Airport (CO)
Phase of Flight:	Climb (3,000' AGL)
Effect on Flight:	Precautionary landing
Damage:	Nose, engines 1 and 2
Wildlife Species:	American white pelicans
Comments from Report:	Shortly after departure, the aircraft had multiple, large birdstrikes. One bird penetrated the nose area just below the windshield and continued through the forward cockpit bulkhead. Bird remains were sprayed throughout the cockpit. No injuries reported. Both engines ingested at least 1 bird. The #1 engine had fan damage: the #2 engine lost power and had a dented inlet lip. ID by Smithsonian, Division of Birds. NTSB investigated. Cost reported to exceed $2 million.

Date:	19 April 2008
Aircraft:	Piper Aerostar
Airport:	Colorado Springs Airport (CO)
Phase of Flight:	Approach (2,000' AGL)
Effect on Flight:	Emergency landing
Damage:	Windshield
Wildlife Species:	Turkey vulture
Comments from Report:	Bird penetrated center of front windshield when aircraft was on 10-mile final leaving a 2-ft hole. Pilot was injured, his headset was knocked off. Vision was impaired by blood and the 200 mph wind coming through the broken windshield. Pilot was unable to directly communicate with the tower but transponded an emergency signal hoping the control tower would clear the airport for him. An uneventful landing was made. Pilot was treated at hospital.

Date:	2 May 2008
Aircraft:	RV-7A
Airport:	Frazier Lake Airpark (CA)
Phase of Flight:	Climb (50' AGL)
Effect on Flight:	Crashed
Damage:	Destroyed
Wildlife Species:	Canada goose
Comments from Report:	During departure for a touch and go landing, aircraft hit a goose with the left wing. Pilot lost control and crashed into a field 500 feet southwest of the runway and cart wheeled. The aircraft was destroyed. NTSB investigated.

Date:	25 May 2008
Aircraft:	B-747-200
Airport:	Brussels Intl. Airport (Belgium)
Phase of Flight:	Takeoff run
Effect on Flight:	Aborted takeoff
Damage:	Aircraft destroyed
Wildlife Species:	Eurasian kestrel
Comments from Report:	The aircraft overran the runway after a rejected takeoff due to a bird being ingested in #3 engine. The plane broke into three pieces. None of the five on board was seriously injured. ID by Smithsonian, Division of Birds (U.S. air carrier).

Date:	27 May 2008
Aircraft:	B-737-200
Airport:	Ugnu-Kuparuk Airport (AK)
Phase of Flight:	Approach (500' AGL)
Effect on Flight:	Aborted landing
Damage:	Engine
Wildlife Species:	Trumpeter swan
Comments from Report:	During approach, a trumpeter swan was ingested. Pilot aborted landing at Kuparuk. Engine was shut down and secured. The flight diverted to Deadhorse without further incident. Cost of repairs was $500,000. Time out of service was 3 days.

Date:	9 June 2008
Aircraft:	BE-58
Airport:	Hernando Village Airpark (MS)
Phase of Flight:	Climb (rotation)
Effect on Flight:	Precautionary landing
Damage:	Engine and landing gear
Wildlife Species:	White-tailed deer
Comments from Report:	At rotation, aircraft hit a deer with the right engine, removing the right gear from the aircraft. Aircraft returned to land on the nose gear and left gear. Aircraft skidded off runway. Substantial damage was reported.

Date:	20 June 2008
Aircraft:	B-747-400
Airport:	Chicago O'Hare Intl. (IL)
Phase of Flight:	Takeoff run
Effect on Flight:	Precautionary landing
Damage:	Engine #2
Wildlife Species:	Red-tailed hawk
Comments from Report:	During takeoff run, aircraft ingested a hawk. The flight continued takeoff and climbed to dump 165,000 lbs of fuel (cost $100,000) then returned to the airport with one engine out. Several blades had significant damage. Both the #1 and #2 engines had vibrations but the #1 engine was not damaged. Some blades were replaced while others were blended. Thirty man-hours to repair.

Date:	5 July 2008
Aircraft:	Mooney M20K
Airport:	Livingston County Spencer J Hardy (MI)
Phase of Flight:	Takeoff run
Effect on Flight:	Aborted takeoff
Damage:	Wing, fuselage, propeller, landing gear
Wildlife Species:	White-tailed deer
Comments from Report:	Aircraft hit a deer on takeoff roll at dusk. The pilot immediately aborted the takeoff and returned to the ramp. The left wing, lower fuselage, propeller and left main landing gear were damaged. NTSB investigated.

Date:	24 July 2008
Aircraft:	Learjet 60
Airport:	Morristown Muni (NJ)
Phase of Flight:	Takeoff run
Effect on Flight:	Aborted takeoff
Damage:	Engine #2 and wing
Wildlife Species:	Canada goose
Comments from Report:	During takeoff run a flock of 2-10 geese were struck. The #2 engine ingested a Canada goose causing damage and the wing was also damaged. Takeoff was aborted. Aircraft was out of service for 8 days and cost totaled $3 million.

Date:	29 August 2008
Aircraft:	Ercoupe 415 C
Airport:	Sebring Regional (FL)
Phase of Flight:	Climb (1,300' AGL)
Effect on Flight:	Engine shut down, emergency landing
Damage:	Destroyed
Wildlife Species:	Unknown bird
Comments from Report:	The pilot saw wood pieces from his prop and white feathers coming into the cockpit through the open canopy. An extreme vibration ensued and he shut the engine down and made an emergency landing in a pasture. The aircraft hit a ditch which was hidden by tall grass. The nose gear collapsed, the right wing spar bent aft and the firewall buckled. The pilot was flying over a garbage dump at the time of the strike. NTSB investigated.

Date:	11 September 2008
Aircraft:	MD-88
Airport:	Atlanta Intl. (GA)
Phase of Flight:	Climb (5' AGL)
Effect on Flight:	Engine shut down, precautionary landing
Damage:	Engine #1
Wildlife Species:	Rock pigeon
Comments from Report:	The number 1 engine was totaled. Odor and haze in cabin. Vibration in engine. Two-ten birds reported as struck. Aircraft made an emergency landing. ID by Smithsonian, Division of Birds. Remains taken from nose and runway.

Date:	21 September 2008
Aircraft:	B-767
Airport:	Orlando Intl. (FL)
Phase of Flight:	Climb (1,000 AGL)
Effect on Flight:	Emergency landing
Damage:	Engine, nose
Wildlife Species:	Wood stork

Comments from Report: Aircraft had multiple birdstrikes shortly after liftoff which hit the left engine and radome. The crew declared an emergency and returned to land safely 12 minutes after departure. Passengers heard 2 loud bangs followed by vibration and noise. A horrible smell was noticed. ID by Smithsonian, Division of Birds.

Date:	26 September 2008
Aircraft:	Cirrus CR-22
Airport:	Fort Lauderdale Executive (FL)
Phase of Flight:	Climb (2,500' AGL)
Effect on Flight:	Emergency landing
Damage:	Windshield, nose, propeller, landing gear
Wildlife Species:	Anhinga

Comments from Report: The bird entered the cockpit, striking the pilot's face. He required stitches. The deice boot on two prop blades received damage. The left engine cowl had damaged paint and fiberglass. ID by Smithsonian, Division of Birds.

Date:	28 September 2008
Aircraft:	Piper 28
Airport:	Beverly Municipal (MA)
Phase of Flight:	Landing roll
Effect on Flight:	None
Damage:	Destroyed
Wildlife Species:	White-tailed deer

Comments from Report: The deer was hit at dusk. The right wing and right engine compartment were severely damaged. Aircraft was considered totaled ($48,000). NTSB investigated.

Date:	25 October 2008
Aircraft:	MD-90-30
Airport:	Salt Lake City (UT)
Phase of Flight:	Takeoff run
Effect on Flight:	Aborted takeoff
Damage:	Engine
Wildlife Species:	Ferruginous hawk (juvenile)

Comments from Report: Hawk was ingested at high speed during takeoff. The engine stalled, lost thrust and takeoff was aborted. Runway was closed 30 minutes for cleanup. Airline mechanics reported that the cost of 4 tires, 4 brake assemblies and 4 fan blades would be $554,400. This cost does not include labor and down time. Flight was delayed 3 hours. Final estimate for repairs was around $3.2 million. Airline policy required pilots be removed from service. ID by Wildlife Services biologist.

Date:	18 November 2008
Aircraft:	Aerospatiale AS 350
Airport:	Near West Point over Hudson River (NY)
Phase of Flight:	En Route (2,000' AGL)
Effect on Flight:	Precautionary landing
Damage:	Canopy and nose
Wildlife Species:	Canada goose
Comments from Report:	Helicopter was over the Hudson River near West Point Military Academy. Report indicates a hole in center left nose area about 21" by 14". New canopy was ordered from France. Cost reported as over $91,000. Time out of service was about 3 months.

Date:	18 November 2008
Aircraft:	MD-11
Airport:	Memphis Intl. (TN)
Phase of Flight:	Climb (100' AGL)
Effect on Flight:	Precautionary landing
Damage:	Engine
Wildlife Species:	Unknown bird
Comments from Report:	At approximately 100' AGL engine had a compressor stall and aircraft yawed left. Pilots heard a loud bang and saw the EVM Comp indicator spike. They made a precautionary landing back at Memphis. Maintenance found moderate damage to the #1 engine. Cost of repairs was $235,000. Time out of service was 41 hours.

Date:	20 November 2008
Aircraft:	B-757-200
Airport:	Chicago O'Hare Intl. (IL)
Phase of Flight:	Climb (2,000' AGL)
Effect on Flight:	Precautionary landing
Damage:	Engine
Wildlife Species:	Mallard
Comments from Report:	During climb-out, pilots felt a bump, heard a bang and smelled something burning. An emergency was declared and an uneventful landing was made. Pilots thought it might have been a birdstrike but were concerned mostly about the smell. Multiple birds were struck. Maintenance found feathers in the fan. Several fan blades were replaced. ID by Smithsonian, Division of Birds.

Date:	6 December 2008
Aircraft:	A-320
Airport:	New Orleans Intl. (LA)
Phase of Flight:	Climb (500' AGL)
Effect on Flight:	Engine shut down and precautionary landing
Damage:	Engine
Wildlife Species:	Lesser scaup
Comments from Report:	During climb-out, 4 birds appeared on the nose out of the dark. Birds tried to dive and were lost from view on right side followed by a loud thump and #2 engine vibrations. An emergency was declared and a/c returned to land. Post flight inspection found major engine damage. There were many deformed fan and exhaust blades. ID by Smithsonian, Division of Birds.

Date:	19 December 2008
Aircraft:	MD-10-10
Airport:	Memphis Intl. (TN)
Phase of Flight:	Approach (2,700' AGL)
Effect on Flight:	None
Damage:	Engine, engine cowl, thrust reverser
Wildlife Species:	Gadwall
Comments from Report:	Replaced #3 engine cowl, #3 engine and #3 thrust reverser. Time out of service was 78 hours. Total cost was $913,678. ID by Smithsonian, Division of Birds.

Date:	26 December 2008
Aircraft:	DC-10-30
Airport:	Memphis Intl. (TN)
Phase of Flight:	Descent (9,700' AGL)
Effect on Flight:	None
Damage:	Wing
Wildlife Species:	Snow goose
Comments from Report:	Repaired and replaced two slats. Time out of service was 8 days. Costs totaled $220,000. ID by Smithsonian, Division of Birds.

These turkey vultures were attracted to the carcass of a Canada goose at the approach end of a runway at an eastern U.S. airport, March 2008. The goose had been struck by a landing aircraft 1 hour earlier. Carcasses at airports not only pose a direct foreign object damage (FOD) hazard, but they attract scavenging birds and mammals as well. Carcasses from wildlife strikes should be removed from the air operations area as soon as possible. Photo by USDA.